Just when it seemed that the subject of the American Revolution had been thoroughly explored, Richard Borkow has given us a fresh look at the war's culminating event—the 1781 march of French and American troops to Virginia.

—Joseph Wheelan, author of *Jefferson's War: America's First War on Terror, 1801–1805*, and *Mr. Adams's Last Crusade: John Quincy Adams's Extraordinary Post-Presidential Life in Congress*

Dobbs Ferry Road to Freedom Walk, August 19, 2007, led by Hugh Francis, reenacting George Washington on horseback. *Copyright by Anne Marie Leone. 2007; published by permission.*

GEORGE WASHINGTON'S

Westchester

GAMBLE

The Encampment on the Hudson
& the Trapping of Cornwallis

RICHARD BORKOW

THE
History
PRESS

Published by The History Press
Charleston, SC 29403
www.historypress.net

Front cover: Detail from *Redoubt, Dobbs Ferry*, Jasper F. Cropsey, 1892. *Collection of the Newington-Cropsey Foundation.*

First published 2011

Manufactured in the United States

ISBN 978.1.60949.039.3

Library of Congress Cataloging-in-Publication Data
Borkow, Richard.
George Washington's Westchester gamble : the encampment on the Hudson and the
trapping of Cornwallis / Richard Borkow.
p. cm.
Includes bibliographical references and index.
ISBN 978-1-60949-039-3
1. New York (State)--History--Revolution, 1775-1783--Campaigns. 2. United States--History-
-Revolution, 1775-1783--Campaigns. 3. Hudson River Valley (N.Y. and N.J.)--History,
Military--18th century. 4. Washington, George, 1732-1799--Military leadership. I. Title.
E230.5.N4B67 2011
974.7'03--dc22
2011009604

*This book is dedicated
to the memory of the late Senator Craig Thomas of Wyoming,
with gratitude to him for his commitment to a faithful account
of the Washington-Rochambeau National Historic Trail.*

I have pondered over the toils that were endured by the officers and soldiers of the army who achieved...independence.

I have often inquired of myself, what great principle or idea it was that kept this Confederacy so long together.

It was not the mere matter of the separation of the colonies from the mother land; but something in that Declaration giving liberty, not alone to the people of this country, but hope to the world for all future time...that in due time the weights should be lifted from the shoulders of all men, and that all should have an equal chance.

—Abraham Lincoln, at Independence Hall, Philadelphia, February 22, 1861

CONTENTS

ACKNOWLEDGEMENTS

The gathering of the material for *George Washington's Westchester Gamble* has been part of an effort, now in its sixth year, to collect historical information about the remarkable events that occurred in Dobbs Ferry and neighboring localities in Westchester County, New York, during the Revolutionary War and to make that information available to the general public.

Markers along the way have included the annual celebrations, since 2006, of Dobbs Ferry's Road to Freedom Day, the 2009 publication of *George Washington at Head Quarters, Dobbs Ferry*, by Dr. Mary Sudman Donovan and the posting on YouTube of *Notable Historians Reveal Dobbs Ferry's Historic River Connections*, a video interview project sponsored by the New York Council for the Humanities.[1] Other markers have included efforts to ensure historically accurate representation for Dobbs Ferry and neighboring localities in educational material about the Washington-Rochambeau National Historical Trail and the July 25, 2009 ceremony in Dobbs Ferry, sponsored by the Hudson River Valley National Heritage Area, to welcome French Ambassador Pierre Vimont and to celebrate passage of the legislation that created the Washington-Rochambeau National Historical Trail.

The backing from public officials and from the community as a whole on behalf of these endeavors has been amazing and truly gratifying.

Special acknowledgment is due to Dobbs Ferry's representatives in Congress, and my heartfelt thanks go to Congresswoman Nita Lowey, whose commitment to integrity and unstinting support have been magnificent and whose generous assistance is deeply appreciated, and to Congressman Eliot Engel, whose help during the legislative process was extremely timely and invaluable.

Many thanks to Town of Greenburgh Supervisor Paul Feiner, who has a deep interest in the history of Greenburgh and who has been constantly encouraging and supportive. Assemblyman Tom Abinanti and Senator Andrea Stewart-Cousins have been very much involved in our programs and have rendered important assistance at the county and state levels. Dobbs Ferry Mayor Hartley Connett and former Dobbs Ferry Mayors Scott Seskin and Joseph Bova have been key players and strong supporters at all the critical junctures, as have all the trustees of the Village of Dobbs Ferry. It has been a pleasure and an honor to have their bipartisan backing. I am obliged to village trustees David Koenigsberg and the late Larry Dengler, both also historical society trustees, and both of whom, from the start of this effort in 2006, again and again offered help in multiple ways.

The very existence of this historical program is a tribute to the unflagging energy and enthusiasm of all the trustees of the Dobbs Ferry Historical Society, and I am eternally indebted to them for what they have done. The trustees of the historical society initiated Road to Freedom Day, and the success and fun of our pageantry and celebrations are due to them.

Historians David Hackett Fischer and Thomas Fleming have made significant contributions to this project. It has been an enormous benefit to be able to rely on their expertise, which they have generously offered. I have been fortunate in my contacts and discussions with other historians as well, including Barnet Schecter, Joseph Wheelan, James Johnson and Robert Selig, and I thank them for sharing their thoughts with me and for their kind suggestions. The highly capable staff at the Westchester County Archives in Elmsford, New York, have also provided invaluable guidance, for which I am very grateful.

Throughout the process of writing *George Washington's Westchester Gamble* I have had the great advantage of working with Whitney Tarella, my editor at The History Press. It has been an extremely enjoyable relationship, and Whitney's excellent advice has rescued me more than once! My copyeditor at The History Press, Hilary McCullough, has added insightful recommendations and shepherded me expertly through the final stages of manuscript preparation.

I am very grateful to all the persons mentioned above. But the guidance given by one individual, my life partner, Linda Borkow, stands out most of all. This project really belongs as much to her as to me, and I can never adequately express my appreciation to her for her constant dedication. It simply would have been impossible to proceed without her insight, her encouragement and her love.

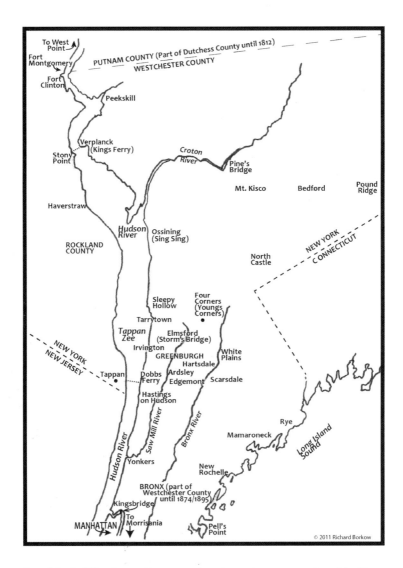

Localities in Westchester County and environs that are mentioned in *George Washington's Westchester Gamble.*

Introduction

CHANGING SCENES
OF WAR

THE NORTH RIVER

SEPTEMBER AND OCTOBER 1776: A CONNECTICUT YANKEE BENEATH KING GEORGE'S SHIPS

On a day in late summer 1776, David Bushnell's *American Turtle*, the world's first submarine, was placed on a sloop at Dobbs Ferry and conveyed down the Hudson River—it was usually called the North River then—toward New York Harbor.[2] The date was September 6, and the United States was only two months old. The war in Westchester County had begun in earnest in July when two British warships, the *Phoenix* and the *Rose*, sailed north from New York Harbor, mocked the ineffectual fire from American posts on the river and penetrated into the Tappan Zee. There they remained for more than a month, flaunting British naval power and asserting British domination of the waters around New York. The *American Turtle*'s objective was a bold one: to challenge British naval effrontery by destroying King George's warships in New York Harbor.

Bushnell, the inventor and builder of the submarine, was a Connecticut Yankee, a farmer's son and a mechanical genius. When the war broke out at

Lexington and Concord in April 1775, he decided to apply his engineering talents to the defense of New England liberties. The British fleet that controlled the waters of Boston Harbor gave the enemy an enormous advantage. Bushnell reasoned that a submergible vessel, armed with an explosive charge, might reduce that advantage, and he set to work. In the construction of the *Turtle*, the only assistance he received was from his brother, Ezra.

As an initial step, he demonstrated for the first time that a charge of powder could explode underwater. He called the charge a "torpedo," adapting the term from the name of the stinging fish torpedinidae.[3] The brothers then proceeded to build the submarine, which would have room for a single operator.

The workmanship was masterful. The brothers joined the wooden planks that constituted the walls of the vessel, making watertight seals; they conceived of the many appurtenances that would be needed, including the brass cover, which provided space for the operator's head, and the glass eyes that enabled the operator to see underwater. They designed the steerage mechanism, a kind of corkscrew that allowed both forward and backward movement of the submarine, and they invented mechanisms that would allow fresh air to enter and consumed air to be flushed out. Much like a modern submarine, the entry of water caused it to submerge, and the expulsion of water, to resurface. But it took quite a while to build. By the time the brothers were finished, Washington had been able to oust the British army from Boston and the British fleet from Boston Harbor.

King George's warships did not stay away from American waters for very long. In July 1776, a huge number appeared in the lower harbor of New York and disembarked tens of thousands of troops, unopposed, onto Staten Island. It was the largest expeditionary force that Great Britain had ever assembled to send to war.

Accordingly, David Bushnell now turned his attention to New York Harbor. He landed the *American Turtle* at New Rochelle and took it cross county in a wagon to the Hudson River at Dobbs Ferry. Bushnell had received permission from General Washington to put his submarine into action. Nevertheless, the commander in chief was skeptical; he agreed to give the *American Turtle* a trial, but only at the importuning of Governor Trumbull of Connecticut.

The operator for the mission on September 6 was Eli Lee, a strong, young Connecticut man. Strength would be important because the vessel was propelled underwater exclusively by muscle power. The sloop from Dobbs Ferry entered New York Harbor and, as closely as it dared, approached some of the larger ships. Then the *Turtle*, with Eli inside, plunged into the water. Submerged and out of sight, he came up to the HMS *Eagle*. The plan was to attach the torpedo to the hull of the ship. Eli's attempt probably would have succeeded if the attachment site had been wood. But copper plating foiled his efforts, and he did not have enough muscular endurance to stay submerged and try again. Coming to the surface, he was spotted by more than one hundred British troops standing on a parapet. Puzzled by what they saw, not knowing what to make of it, they didn't interfere. Several minutes later, Eli released the torpedo into the river: it caused a massive explosion, but no damage, and he was able to get himself to Manhattan (still in American hands on September 6) and safety.

In October 1776, near the shoreline of Dobbs Ferry, the British took their revenge on the *American Turtle*. This was the month when the war became intense in Westchester County, culminating in the Battle of White Plains on October 28. As a preliminary thrust (or perhaps a feint) in the Westchester County campaign, British warships on October 9 threatened to land at Dobbs Ferry, and Washington, at his headquarters on Harlem Heights, became alarmed. An American force was immediately dispatched to Dobbs Ferry to repel the invaders. According to the memoirs of General William Heath:

> [Oct] *9: Early in the morning, three* [British] *ships...* [came] *up the...*
> *River...two* [American] *galleys* [were forced to shore] *near Dobbs'*
> *Ferry. The enemy...landed a number of men, who plundered a store...*
> *The General ordered Col. Sargeant, with 500 infantry, 40 light horse...*
> [and] *artillery...to march immediately, with all possible expedition, to*
> *Dobbs' Ferry. The enemy...sunk a sloop which had onboard the machine*
> *invented by Mr. Bushnell...its fate was truly a contrast to its design.*[4]

Accounts differ on what happened next. Apparently, David Bushnell claimed that he was able to recover the *American Turtle* from the bottom of the Hudson.[5] Yet no one saw him dredge it up to shore, and after it was sunk, the *Turtle* was never seen again. Washington Irving, who describes the *Turtle*'s career in some detail, writes only that the submarine sank to the bottom of the river and says nothing about its recovery—by Bushnell or by anyone else.

There is reason to question whether the *American Turtle* was dredged up from the bottom of the river. True, Bushnell was an extraordinarily talented engineer. But to recover the submarine from the bottom of the river during wartime with enemy ships dominating the waters, and to accomplish this feat unobserved, seems to be beyond even David Bushnell's capabilities. This was an era before patent protection, and Bushnell was very secretive about his submarine. He was determined to prevent others from stealing the design. Bushnell was also rather reclusive by nature and in his later years, for reasons that are not entirely clear, decided to make his past obscure. He no longer answered to the name of David Bushnell, referring to himself, instead, as "Dr. Bush."[6]

Did David Bushnell claim that he had recovered the *American Turtle* because he feared that someone else would, in the future, try to do exactly that, succeed in bringing it to shore and copy his engineering design? If he did not truly recover it, the world's first submarine may still be at the bottom of the Hudson, near the shores of Dobbs Ferry.

View of the Hudson River from Dobbs Ferry. *Author's photo.*

Dobbs Ferry: November 1777

"A Brutal and Cruel Attack"[7]

When the career of the *American Turtle* came to an end, Westchester County was about to enter a new and terrible stage of war. In the months prior to the *Turtle*, the main weapons of conflict in the county had been pamphlets, filled either with anti-Whig or anti-Tory invective. While comity had suffered, lives and property had been spared. The new stage would spare neither. It began with the battles of Pell's Point in mid-October 1776 and of White Plains on October 28.

Following the Battle of White Plains, the contending armies withdrew to more secure lines, the Americans north to Peekskill and the British south to Kingsbridge. Most of the residents of Westchester County had the misfortune to reside in the area that lay between, the "neutral ground." It was so named because the main armies, for the most part, did not attempt to occupy it. The area's "neutrality" did not protect the population, however, who suffered from repeated raids.

In the autumn of 1777, one year after the sinking of the *American Turtle*, the British seized major forts in the lower Hudson valley and became the dominant military presence in the region, emboldening Loyalist raiders.[8] It was a time for Patriots residing in the neutral ground to proceed cautiously. Prudent Whigs understood that it was wise to avoid provocations and lie low. Ignoring those considerations, three young men on the Dobbs Ferry Road (now Ashford Avenue), a short distance west of the Saw Mill River, summoned the nerve to confront a small number of mounted Loyalist militiamen and to rebuke them in some fashion. Exactly what form the rebuke took, we do not know. The descriptions that have come down to us indicate that the young men, whose names were Barton, Lawrence Smith and Vincent, taunted the Tories. The accounts agree that what followed was an exceedingly brutal affair.

The Loyalists in this instance were identified as members of Kipp's mounted regiment, one of several marauding bands that plagued Westchester County during the war. Enraged by the taunting, Kipp's horsemen fell upon the three young men, beating them mercilessly. The beatings had a degree of severity and cruelty that seemed to exceed the ordinary brutality and depredations of war: Barton and Lawrence Smith died from the beating within a few days. The third young man, Vincent, survived but suffered with a lifelong disability, for one eyewitness recalled that his skull was split by one of Kipp's men. The community was outraged by this vicious act, and word of the assault spread far, eventually reaching the ears of the Congress, which saw fit to compensate young Vincent with a pension—the first, we are told, ever awarded by the United States.[9]

Storm's Bridge: November 1777

That same month in a separate attack, three miles to the north, a much larger band of Loyalists raided and destroyed the homes of three prominent Patriot citizens, Abraham Storm, Cornelius Van Tassel and his cousin Peter Van Tassel. The native-born Tory raiders, reinforced by Hessian troops, departed on horseback from the Loyalist base camp of Morrisania on the icy cold night of November 16 and arrived at Storm's Bridge (present-day Elmsford) around midnight. The unit was led by Colonel Andreas Emmerich, a redoubtable Loyalist commander, whose name was greatly feared in Westchester County. The militia and dragoons that he headed, known as Emmerich's (or Emmerick's) Chasseurs, were skilled at capturing Patriot leaders.

On this occasion, the raiders were looking primarily for the Van Tassels and for as many Van Tassel confederates as they could find. The day before, Emmerich had sought permission for the raid from his superior, William Tryon: "Sir, I am intending to make a march to Morrow Night at the Hour of Six, so that with Your Excellency's approbation, I with my Company may be at VAN TASSEL's House by Two oClock the following Morning, where there is a pretty Large Nest of Rebels...I beg Your Excelly. woud. be pleased to Grant me this request, that my People may have a little Work."[10]

While the Van Tassels were the principal targets, the seizure of Abraham Storm would be a bonus. He was the proprietor of a tavern and popular meeting place for Patriot militia at the corner of Sawmill River Road and Tarrytown Road, the main intersection of Storm's Bridge then and the main intersection of Elmsford today. Abraham resided with his family at the tavern. But on that particular night he was not at home. His absence was upsetting, but there was nevertheless work to be done: Emmerich's men looted the tavern and burned most of the building to the ground.

Their work at the tavern completed, the raiders went after the two Van Tassel cousins, who resided a short distance to the south. Unluckily, both were in their houses that night, and both were captured by the raiders. After seizing them, the Loyalists and Hessians were, of course, not finished, for according to standard practice, they were entitled to all the plunder that they could find. They scoured the two homes for valuables, while the terrified wives and children of Peter and Cornelius hid themselves in the old root cellar or in outdoor sheds. After collecting their loot, the raiders set fire to the houses.

The raiders were not without humanity: a Hessian soldier found Cornelius's infant daughter, Leah, still in the house and, at some risk to himself, ignoring the smoke and flames, was able to rescue Leah and give the infant to her distraught mother.

Cornelius's teenage son, Cornelius Jr., who was also still inside the house when it was set afire, managed to escape by jumping from the roof into the yard, which was crowded with Emmerich's men. Cornelius Jr. held a musket and swung it at the raiders, who were taken by surprise by his sudden appearance. Before they could grab him, he sprinted to Saw Mill River and jumped into the ice-cold water.[11] He evaded capture, but he later succumbed to the exposure that he suffered during his escape.

Romer–Van Tassel House on Saw Mill River Road in Elmsford. *Author's photo.*

In 1845, Captain John Romer, who married Leah, explained: "The only son, Cornelius, Jr., fled for safety half naked to the roof of the house and held on by the chimney, from which when the fire began to reach him he jumped to the ground. He escaped that night, but caught cold from which he never recovered."[12]

These incidents are a small sampling of the appalling hardships suffered in Westchester during the war. Roger Jewell, in his *Sawmill River Valley War*, states that in November 1777, the people of the county witnessed the onset of a "Reign of Terror."[13] November 1777 was bad enough. Worse would come in the summer months of 1779, when General Henry Clinton, British commander in New York, unleashed a series of furious attacks against communities in Westchester and against nearby towns on the Connecticut shore of Long Island Sound.

NOVEMBER 1780 AND MARCH 1781: "A COUNTRY IN RUINS"

By 1780, Westchester County was described as a "country in ruins" by Dr. James Thacher, a surgeon in the Continental army and one of the chief chroniclers of the war. He visited the county in November 1780 as part of a foraging party and made these observations:

> *This country...is called the neutral ground, but the miserable inhabitants who remain are not much favored with the privileges which their neutrality ought to secure them...*
> *The country is rich and fertile...but it now has the marks of a country in ruins. A large proportion of the proprietors having abandoned their farms, the few that remain find it impossible to harvest their produce...Banditti, consisting of lawless villains...devote themselves to the most cruel pillage and robbery among the defenseless inhabitants between the lines...These shameless marauders have received the names of Cow-boys and Skinners. By their atrocious deeds they have become a scourge and terror to the people.[14]*

Dr. Thacher added these comments when he visited Westchester once more in March 1781, this time on a medical mission:

We found many friends to our cause, who reside on their farms between the lines of the two armies, whose situation is truly deplorable, being continually exposed to the ravages of the Tories, horse thieves and Cowboys, who rob and plunder them without mercy, and the personal abuse and punishments which they inflict, is almost incredible—the particulars of which have been already noticed.[15]

The Cow-boys were Tory raiders and ostensibly rode under the British banner but were not particularly discriminating in their attacks on civilians and their property. They were one of the two principal marauder bands that plundered Westchester County during the Revolutionary War. The Skinners were the other, ostensibly riding under the American banner. But the Skinners were also non-discriminating in their attacks. As we can see from the quotation above, Dr. Thacher, a man totally committed to the American cause, made no excuses for the Skinners and did not distinguish their lawlessness from that of the Cow-boys. Both were "shameless," both "a scourge and terror to the people."

July 1781: Transformation of the Countryside

Four months later, on July 4–6, 1781, a ten-mile swath of Westchester County was suddenly transformed when Washington's 4,500 Continental troops formed a junction with their French allies, an army of 5,000 men under the command of the Comte de Rochambeau. The two armies had marched to Westchester from different points—the Continental troops from Newburgh, New York, and the French from Newport, Rhode Island—in order to meet in the lower part of the county by the Hudson River and set up a side-by-side encampment.

The Americans were soon deployed on the hilltops of present-day Greenburgh, New York, in Dobbs Ferry and Ardsley. The French regiments bivouacked on the hills to the east of the Americans, some in the Greenburgh localities of Hartsdale and Edgemont and others in White Plains. Separating the two armies was the deep gorge of the Sprain Brook, which is spanned today by the Heatherdell Road overpass near the Ardsley-Hartsdale border.[16]

Dr. Thacher was one of the Americans stationed in Dobbs Ferry and has provided some of the liveliest accounts that we have of major events and prominent personalities of the encampment. He was assigned to Colonel Scammel's light infantry unit, which was stationed on the high ground in the area later known as Echo Hills, in the eastern part of Dobbs Ferry. Children's Village, a residential school for boys, is located on that high ground today. Baron Ludwig von Closen, aide-de-camp to General Rochambeau, also chronicled the events at the encampment, and his diary serves as an invaluable French companion to Thacher's work.[17]

On July 7, the allied armies were reviewed by their commanding generals and on July 10 by the French ambassador to the United States, the Chevalier de la Luzerne, who had just arrived from Philadelphia, the capital of the United States. Since France was the first and, at this point, the only country with an embassy in the American republic, Luzerne (and his secretary, Francois Marbois) constituted Philadelphia's entire diplomatic corps.

The allied armies looked south toward the enemy forces of General Sir Henry Clinton, which controlled New York City and Long Island. Clinton's northern perimeter was at the northwestern tip of Manhattan (Kingsbridge), just twelve miles below the allies.

The side-by-side encampment had been Washington's idea. At a conference with Rochambeau in late May at Wethersfield, Connecticut, the two generals had agreed to bring their two armies into Westchester County and position them in proximity to Sir Henry's forces. Washington's intention was to probe for weaknesses in Clinton's defenses and, if possible, find a way to attack the British garrison on Manhattan.

THE CONCERNS OF THE COMMANDER IN CHIEF

The Lower Westchester Encampment of 1781 transformed much more than the appearance of the countryside. With the establishment of an allied encampment so far to the south, the neutral ground became a small fraction of its former size. It was now extremely difficult for Tory raiding parties from below to enter the area, and the security of the population, which had been terribly compromised for years, was suddenly and dramatically improved.

The security gains of the distressed people of the county were gratifying. But the commander in chief was focused on wider concerns in the summer of 1781 when he brought the allied armies to Westchester County. The long and seemingly inconclusive war was already in its seventh year, and the opposing sides, to all appearances, were locked in stalemate. Ambassador Luzerne had made it clear to Congress more than a year before that French support could not be provided indefinitely and that the campaign of 1781 would almost certainly be the last.[18]

Since that warning, the situation had only become worse. "The friends of America," John Adams reported from Europe, "trembled… at the current abasement" of the United States.[19] Why they trembled is not hard to discover: through 1780 and the first half of 1781, Europe received one gloomy report after another from the United States— colossal defeats in the South at Charleston and Camden; the collapse of the American currency; the treason of one of Washington's most capable generals; mutinies in the Continental army. As the bad news poured in, the conclusion seemed unavoidable: the Americans were incapable of reaching their goal of a free, independent republic.

If the stalemate were not broken soon, if the war did not end with an unambiguous military victory, then it would come to an end in another way—through mediation by the great powers. Under those circumstances, the American states could expect to face a highly unfavorable ceasefire arrangement, imposed by despots of central and eastern Europe, at a proposed conference in Vienna.

The overall prospects for the United States therefore seemed grim when Washington and Rochambeau entered Westchester County early in the summer of 1781, and few imagined that 1781 could be the year of a significant battlefield triumph. Yet three months later, the French and American armies, in cooperation with a powerful French fleet, won a major victory at Yorktown, Virginia, by defeating Lord Cornwallis, Earl of Eyre, and his 7,500 British and Hessian troops. The victory at Yorktown led to the end of the war, to uncontested independence for the United States and to remarkably favorable peace terms for our young republic.

How was such a dramatic turnaround achieved? To answer that question, we need to look at the crucial decisions that were made during the sixth week of the Lower Westchester Encampment, in mid-August

1781, by Generals Washington and Rochambeau, when they risked everything on a march south and designed the strategy that would win the war. We also need to look at the history of the American and French alliance, for France was America's indispensable ally when the thirteen United States won their independence. The turnaround in the fortunes of the United States was based on a French partnership that had been evolving for many years.

Themes of the Chapters

Chapter 1, "The American Revolution and Its Early French Connections," sketches out the first attempts of the Americans and the French to explore the possibility of a military relationship. The chapter also deals with the single most important figure to contribute to that relationship, the Marquis de Lafayette.

Chapter 2, "Turning Point on the Hudson: Victory at Saratoga Leads to the French Alliance," describes the strategic importance of the Hudson River, Great Britain's effort to seize control of the Hudson and the resulting Battle of Saratoga, north of Albany. The stunning American victory at Saratoga (October 1777) brought an end to the surreptitious phase of the partnership between France and the United States and led to an open military alliance between the two countries (February 1778).

Chapter 3, "Rochambeau's Arrival and Arnold's Treason," carries the French partnership forward into 1780 and describes key moments of Benedict Arnold's treason. Because of coincident timing, Arnold's betrayal threatened the safety of General Rochambeau's newly arrived army at Newport, Rhode Island.

Chapter 4, "Episodes from the War in Westchester," connects military actions in the county to the wider national conflict and shows how a series of local clashes in Westchester constituted a war within a war.

Chapter 5, "Now or Never Our Deliverance Must Come," brings the conflict into the desperate early months of 1781, when mutiny roiled the Continental army, collapse of the currency undermined the country's economy and impending mediation in Vienna threatened to impose highly unfavorable terms on the young American confederation.

Chapter 6, "To New York or to Virginia?," deals with the Washington-Rochambeau conference at Wethersfield, Connecticut, in late May 1781, the decisions made at Wethersfield that led to the Lower Westchester Encampment and the internal communications of the American, French and British high commands in May, June and July 1781, which contributed to the eventual trapping of Cornwallis.

Chapter 7, "The Encampment by the Hudson," describes the side-by-side encampment of the American and French armies in July and August 1781 on the hilltops of lower Westchester from Dobbs Ferry into White Plains and links the deployment sites of 1781 with present-day locations. The Lower Westchester Encampment was the scene for General Washington's high-risk gamble of mid-August 1781.

Chapter 8, "George Washington's Westchester Gamble," shows how the American commander in chief risked all when he broke camp in lower Westchester and ordered a march of the American and French armies from the Hudson River to the Chesapeake region of Virginia, a distance of more than four hundred miles. The chapter concludes with the pivotal second Battle of the Capes and the Franco-American victory over Cornwallis at Yorktown.

The Epilogue portrays the consequences of the Franco-American victory at Yorktown, the impact in Parliament of Cornwallis's defeat and the peace treaty negotiations in Paris. Sadly, until the terms of the treaty were settled and the articles of peace ratified, the war went on, and in Westchester and in other zones of conflict there were continuing clashes and continuing casualties.

THE PHILIPSBURG ENCAMPMENT

The "Lower Westchester Encampment" of 1781 has traditionally been known as the "Philipsburg Encampment." In this book, Lower Westchester is used as the name for the encampment rather than Philipsburg, since the latter term is unfamiliar to the general public and is likely to be confusing to the historic tourist.

Lower Westchester is also a more accurate geographic designation than is Philipsburg. The allied encampment of

1781 extended east of the Bronx River, but Philipsburg did not. Important components of the encampment that were not deployed in Philipsburg but east of the Bronx River included the Legion de Lauzun, commanded by the celebrated Duc de Lauzun, which was stationed in White Plains, and Colonel David Waterbury's 5th Connecticut regiment, which was stationed near the present-day White Plains–Scarsdale border.

Philipsburg, or the "Manor of Philipsburg," took its name from the immensely wealthy Philipse family, whose patriarch at the outbreak of the war was Frederick Philipse III (the "lord of the manor").[20] His principal residence was at Philipse Manor Hall, which has been preserved as a historic site in downtown Yonkers by New York State.

Philipse was an ardent Tory. Because he was considered a security threat, Washington ordered his arrest in 1776, and he was brought to Connecticut, where he was held for several months. Washington then released him and allowed him to return to Yonkers on "parole" (his pledge not to defect to the British or give them material aid). Philipse soon broke his parole by crossing into British-controlled Manhattan, where he remained for the duration of the war. His property was confiscated by New York State in 1779. When the British army evacuated New York City in 1783, Philipse departed with it and took up residence in England. Under the terms of New York State's Confiscation Act of 1784, much of Philipsburg Manor was sold to its former tenants.

The name Philipsburg was discontinued after the war, and in 1788, in the encampment localities west of the Bronx River, the name Greenburgh was adopted instead. Dobbs Ferry, Ardsley, Hartsdale and Edgemont are all located in the town of Greenburgh.

In his voluminous correspondence from the encampment, Washington refrained from using the name Philipsburg and instead wrote, "Head Quarters, at Dobbs's ferry," "Head Quarters, near Dobbs's ferry" or similar variants as the headings for his letters.

Chapter 1

THE AMERICAN REVOLUTION AND ITS EARLY FRENCH CONNECTIONS

It is not choice then, but necessity, that calls for independence, as the only means by which foreign alliances can be obtained.
—Richard Henry Lee

Why was France willing to deploy a large army, at General Washington's request, in Westchester County during the summer of 1781? Why did France decide to place that army in the United States at all? Why did France do so much to aid the American cause?

The antecedents to those decisions can be found years before, in the early steps that were taken by both France and America to explore the possibility of military cooperation.

1763–1775: COVERTLY, FRANCE MONITORS THE POLITICAL MOOD IN THE THIRTEEN COLONIES

France suffered a humiliating defeat at the hands of the British in the French and Indian War, a humiliation that was codified by the terms of the Treaty of Paris (1763). From the moment the treaty was signed,

France smarted for revenge and looked for ways to turn the tables on the British. The French government was well aware of growing political discontent in the thirteen British colonies in North America. Might the discontent be strong enough to grow into an armed uprising? If a colonial uprising should erupt in British North America, it could only weaken the English enemy and be of benefit to France.

As early as 1763, Etienne-Francois Choiseul, Comte de Stainville, the French foreign minister, was sending covert agents to the British colonies in order to assess the political temper of the Americans. Most prominent among the agents was Baron Johann de Kalb, a French army officer of German background who spent several months in America in 1768 and reported back to the Comte de Stainville that the mood of discontent in the colonies was widespread and serious.[21] When the colonial uprising began at Lexington and Concord in April 1775, Paris was not taken by surprise.

1775, 1776: THE THIRTEEN "UNITED PROVINCES OF NORTH AMERICA" SEEK FRENCH MILITARY ASSISTANCE

In Massachusetts, after Lexington and Concord, the British were besieged in Boston, at first exclusively by New England militia. As it happened, the Second Continental Congress convened in Philadelphia around this time and decided to lend support to the New England militia by encouraging troops from other colonies to join them, designating them all as a "Continental Army" and naming George Washington as its commander (June 15, 1775). Washington quickly traveled from Philadelphia to Cambridge, Massachusetts, to assume command (July 3, 1775).

When Washington took command, only a radical faction of the Continental Congress was urging a policy of total independence from Great Britain. Still, the Americans seemed to feel that they constituted at least a proto-nation, for they fought under a newly created flag, with thirteen red and white alternating stripes, and adopted a distinctive name to describe their union, the United Provinces of North America. Symbolically, by retaining the king's colors in the flag's upper left sector, they simultaneously signaled a desire to preserve a political connection with Great Britain.

By forming a Continental army, the Congress was showing determination to use force in order to resist British domination. At the same time, the delegates were realistic enough to recognize that the thirteen united provinces, by themselves, did not have the wherewithal to overcome the military might of Great Britain. Foreign assistance would be essential if armed resistance were to succeed. While that assistance might perhaps be obtained from the Republic of the United Netherlands or from Spain, it was obvious to the delegates that the foreign power most likely to help was Britain's traditional enemy, France. Congress proceeded to seek French aid by sending its representative, Connecticut lawyer and merchant Silas Deane, to Paris in order to appeal to the French court of Louis XVI for military support. Deane arrived in Paris in the spring of 1776 and sought out the recently appointed French foreign minister, Charles Vergennes.[22]

The siege of Boston continued under Washington's direction and lasted for ten months. It came to an end in March 1776 when, over the course of a single night, Washington's troops placed a battery of cannon on Dorchester Heights, within cannonade range of Boston and the enemy fleet in Boston Harbor. The British position had suddenly become untenable, and they were forced to evacuate. In Paris, news of the British evacuation of Boston evoked joyful street demonstrations as ordinary citizens celebrated the humiliation of France's arch enemy.[23] The government in Paris had further confirmation of popular support in France for the American rebellion.

WHY SHOULD WE BE SO FOND OF CALLING OURSELVES DUTIFUL SUBJECTS OF GREAT BRITAIN? IF WE CONTINUE IN THAT MODE, WHY WOULD THE COURT OF FRANCE TAKE NOTICE OF US?

As the Congressional delegates considered their situation, it seemed that France would be far more likely to provide aid if the thirteen provinces were to drop the ambiguities about separation from Great Britain and declare themselves to be thirteen sovereign independent states. George Wythe, a Virginian, and one of the most thoughtful and eloquent delegates, asked his colleagues to reflect on these questions:

In what character shall we treat?—As subjects of Great Britain,—as rebels? Why should we be so fond of calling ourselves dutiful subjects? If we should offer our trade to the court of France, would they take notice of it any more than if Bristol or Liverpool should offer theirs, while we profess to be subjects?...If we were to tell them that, after a season, we would return to our subjection to Great Britain, would not a foreign court wish something more permanent? [24]

Sentiment was shifting away from support for humble petitions to the king and toward increased defiance. Thomas Paine's *Common Sense* (published January 1776), with its soaring advocacy of liberty and utter contempt for tyrannical rule, had a major impact on public opinion. The rumor that the British government had hired Hessian and other German mercenaries to join the British army in subjugating America inflamed passions even more. Among the many factors affecting the delegates, however, it was George Wythe's practical point that ultimately carried the day: military assistance from abroad was essential and would be difficult to obtain unless the American Congress insisted upon independence and vowed never to return to British rule.

On June 2, 1776, another Virginian, Richard Henry Lee, put the case emphatically in a letter that he wrote to Landon Carter:

The infamous treaties with Hesse, Brunswick etc. of which we have authentic copies...leaves not a doubt but that our enemies are determined upon the absolute conquest and subduction of N. America. It is not choice then, but necessity that calls for independence, as the only means by which foreign alliances can be obtained. [25]

Free and Independent States

The time was ripe. On June 7, 1776, Lee presented a resolution to the Congress, perhaps the most momentous that any American Congress has ever been asked to consider:

That these United Colonies are, and of right ought to be, free and independent states, that they are absolved from all allegiance to the British Crown, and that all political connection between them and the State of Great Britain is, and ought to be, totally dissolved.

That it is expedient forthwith to take the most effectual measures for forming foreign Alliances.

That a plan of confederation be prepared and transmitted to the respective Colonies for their consideration and approbation.

Debate followed, and the opponents of independence tried to delay passage of Lee's resolution. But four weeks later they were compelled to yield, and on July 2, 1776, the resolution carried. On July 4, 1776, Congress attempted to show "a decent respect to the opinions of

Monument at site of Old White Plains Court House (on South Broadway) where the Declaration of Independence was first publicly proclaimed, "with beat of drum," by New York State on July 11, 1776. *Author's photo.*

mankind" by endorsing the Declaration of Independence and explaining "the causes that impel them to the separation."

DECEMBER 1776: BENJAMIN FRANKLIN GOES TO PARIS

Congress decided to strengthen its delegation in Paris by sending the renowned Benjamin Franklin to join Deane as a second envoy. When Franklin arrived in France in December 1776, the outpouring of popular affection for the famous New World philosopher and scientist was astonishing. The appreciation shown for Franklin and for the American rebellion that he represented gave the French government confidence that the French people would stand behind an alliance with America.

The court of Louis XVI was very interested in supporting the American uprising militarily, but Foreign Minister Vergennes explained to the American envoys that the assistance would have to be provided secretly. France did not feel ready for war and did not want to provoke Britain. The French government anticipated that war might eventually come, but France first wanted to have the assurance that Spain, the other great Bourbon power, would be an ally in that war. Vergennes assured the American envoys that despite the need for secrecy, abundant French military aid would be sent to America. Indeed, with the assistance of the French playwright Beaumarchais, France arranged to create a bogus Spanish mercantile company, Roderique Hortalez et Cie, which was used to mask the shipping of cannon, ammunition and a whole range of military ordnance to the young republic. (see sidebar "Secrets and Spies" on page 72)

1776: A SHIFTING MILITARY THEATER

With the unambiguous American triumph in Massachusetts in March 1776, the first phase of the war came to an end.[26] During the second phase, which lasted from 1776 to 1779, the main theater would be the middle Atlantic states, where the Americans saw defeat far more often than victory. The preliminaries were in June and July 1776, with the arrival at Staten Island of hundreds of British warships, conveying a huge army of British redcoats and Hessian mercenaries, eventually numbering between thirty and thirty-five thousand men, under the command of two respected military brothers, General William Howe and Admiral Richard Howe.[27] It was the largest expeditionary force that had ever been sent abroad from Great Britain.[28] An American rout at the Battle of Long Island followed in August. Disaster then piled upon disaster, and by early December, after Washington's mortifying retreat across New Jersey, it seemed obvious to most that the rebellion had been defeated.

While the Americans suffered a major loss at the Battle of Long Island, General Howe failed to exploit his advantage fully and missed several opportunities to envelop the American army and destroy it. Had he acted expeditiously on the day of the Battle of Long Island, he could have surrounded the American forts on Brooklyn Heights and captured Washington's entire army. Instead, Washington managed to spirit off the Continental army overnight across the East River to Manhattan from its imperiled position in Brooklyn. An intense fog in the early morning hid the operation during its final stages. Describing the withdrawal of the Americans from Brooklyn, David McCullough writes: "In a single night, 9,000 troops had escaped across the river. Not a life was lost. The only men captured were three who had hung back to plunder."[29] The success of the operation was astonishing, and to some it seemed that the hand of Providence had intervened.[30]

Several days later, General Howe missed a second chance to capture the Continental army when he failed to cut off the American withdrawal from lower to upper Manhattan. A third chance was missed a few weeks after that, during Washington's retreat from Harlem Heights into Westchester County.[31] Had Howe taken advantage of any one of those encirclement opportunities in the vicinity of New York, it is likely that the rebellion would have been crushed. But he did not, and Washington and the Continental army were able to deploy upon the hills surrounding White Plains. There, in early November 1776, the American army, though defeated at the Battle of White Plains, was able to retreat in good order. It deployed in the hilly and relatively secure terrain north of the Croton River. From there, Washington tried to divine Howe's next move. One thing was certain: the Hudson Highlands, the rugged country north of Peekskill on either side of the Hudson River, was a natural fortress that could shelter American troops and must be defended. Peekskill, Washington decided, would serve as headquarters for a Hudson Highlands force of two thousand men under General William Heath.

Later in November, the Americans sustained enormous losses at Fort Washington, in northern Manhattan. Soon after, they lost Fort Lee across the Hudson. The Continental army then retreated across New Jersey, with Washington desperately trying to get his troops to the Delaware River and relative safety in Pennsylvania. As Washington retreated, the British army was in pursuit and close behind but failed to prevent him from reaching the Delaware and crossing the river into Pennsylvania.

Washington Passing the Delaware, 1825, William Humphrys, After: Thomas Sully. Etching and engraving. *Photograph © 2011 Museum of Fine Arts, Boston.*

December 1776 and January 1777: American Triumph in New Jersey

In New Jersey, as the year 1776 came to a close, sentiment swung toward the Tory side, and citizens, encouraged by General Howe, pledged their loyalty to the Crown. Just at this moment of near collapse of the American cause, Washington demonstrated his tenacity, and his proclivity to take unexpected, audacious action, with the American attack and victory at Trenton (December 26). Over the next ten days, Washington's army won a second victory at Trenton and a third at Princeton. The startling triumphs at Trenton and Princeton reversed the mood of despondency in the United States and boosted hope that independence could actually be won on the field of battle.

American morale was so buoyed by the victories in New Jersey, and British morale so shaken, that the British army was forced to pull back from its strongholds in the state and confine itself to a small enclave on the Raritan River between Brunswick and Perth Amboy. The pullback of British troops was hastened by a "forage war" in northern New Jersey, as foraging teams sent out by the British encountered emboldened Americans who met them with force and disrupted their operations. Because of the near total withdrawal of the British army from New Jersey, persons who had pledged loyalty to the king when his army, seemingly invincible, swept through the state two to three months before were abruptly abandoned without protection. It was a pivotal moment of the Revolutionary War.

There would be many American defeats after the triumphs at Trenton and Princeton, and the British would seize many important towns and military posts. But a sea change had occurred. The realists on both sides were starting to conclude that while the British might be able to maintain a hold on important seaports and selected enclaves, America as a whole could not be conquered.

The Marquis de Lafayette

The moment I heard of America, I loved her; the moment I knew she was fighting for freedom, I burnt with a desire of bleeding for her; and the moment I shall be able to serve her at any time, or in any part of the world, will be the happiest one of my life.
—Marquis de Lafayette[32]

According to Lafayette himself, it was a small beginning that led to his involvement in the American War of Independence, an encounter that he had in 1775 with the duke of Gloucester, the younger brother of King George III, while the duke was visiting France.

Marquis de Lafayette, 1788. Laperche. Photograph © 2011 Museum of Fine Arts, Boston.

It is an understatement to say that the royal brothers did not see eye to eye on the conflict in America, for the duke of Gloucester was sympathetic with the American cause and thought that his brother was committing folly by pursuing the war in America.

When Lafayette met the duke, the young marquis was captain of a unit of French dragoons. At dinner with Lafayette and other French officers, the duke of Gloucester must have expressed his support for the Americans in passionate terms. Whatever it was that the duke said, Lafayette recalled later that he had been greatly inspired. "My heart was enlisted," Lafayette wrote about this dinner conversation with the duke, "and I thought only of joining the colors."

Considering Lafayette's accomplishments in America, and the extraordinary impact that he would have, how remarkable were the consequences of this dinner conversation with the brother of King George III!

LAFAYETTE COMES TO AMERICA

Lafayette's actions in support of America began early in 1777 when he was nineteen years old. His parents had died years before, leaving him an inheritance of great wealth and extremely influential connections within the French aristocracy. Lafayette burned with the desire to win fame and glory in America, and he defied both his father-in-law and King Louis XVI when he left France in order to join Washington's army.

While France was eager to weaken Britain by giving aid to the colonial uprising in America, and surreptitiously had been doing exactly that, the French government, in the early part of 1777, did not want to assist the American rebellion openly, fearing that open support might provoke a war with Britain that France was not ready for.

If Lafayette had arranged to travel to America quietly, King Louis XVI would not have objected. But quiet pursuit of glory was not possible for the irrepressible Lafayette. It was important to him that his plans to join Washington's army become widely known. And widely known they did become. The British ambassador to France, Vicount David Murray Stormont, expressed his outrage, threatening that Britain would blockade French ports, for Lafayette had exposed not only his own plans to travel to America but also the similar plans of several other French officers.

Appalled by the turn of events and the possibility that Lafayette's impetuosity might trigger a war between Britain and France, the French government firmly disavowed Lafayette's proposed course of action and forbade French officers from rendering assistance to the Americans.

But Lafayette could not be dissuaded. The sequence of events that finally led to his departure from France is hard to believe: with his own funds, he purchased a ship capable of crossing the Atlantic, evaded a *lettre de cachet* (a royal arrest warrant)[33] and eluded the king's troops, all the while capturing the imagination of the French public. Lafayette's boldness and willingness to take such great risks quickly turned him into a celebrity and a hero.

Word of what the impulsive marquis was doing spread around the country, and people celebrated. In Paris, a mob cheered in the streets. He became an instant hero, a picture of gallant soldiery even before he boarded the ship. Plays were written and performed about his valor. Ambassador Stormont stormed and threatened even more; he honestly reported home the bad news, however, that there was popular opposition in France to the government's attempts to stop Lafayette.[34] Popular approval for the marquis was so intense that the king, in the end, did not press the issue very hard, and many assumed that the government secretly supported his actions.

The American emissaries in Paris, Silas Deane and Benjamin Franklin,[35] were greatly encouraged by the swelling public affection for Lafayette and the unambiguous support of the French people for his actions. The public reaction seemed to reveal not only Lafayette's popularity but also the popularity of the American rebellion. To be sure that Lafayette would have a proper reception when he arrived in America, the emissaries immediately dispatched letters to Congress, explaining that the young marquis was a unique individual of noble lineage, beloved by the French nation, and for that reason, when he arrived in Philadelphia, it was imperative that Congress receive him with appropriate respect and honors. The American emissaries explained:

The Marquis de Lafayette, a young nobleman of great family connections here and great wealth is gone to America in a ship of his own, accompanied by some officers of distinction, in order to serve in our armies. He is exceedingly beloved and everybody's good wishes attend him; we cannot but hope he may meet with such a reception as will make the country and his expedition agreeable to him…we are satisfied that the civilities and respect that may be shown him will be serviceable to our affairs here, as pleasing not only to his powerful relations and to the court but to the whole French nation.[36]

Congress was duly impressed—this was clearly an important young man. When Lafayette arrived in Philadelphia, the delegates appointed him a major general in the American army (thus accepting the high military rank that Silas Deane had already promised him when he was still in France). He was only nineteen years old at the time of the appointment.

LAFAYETTE'S MILITARY CAREER IN AMERICA

Washington quickly took a great liking to the marquis. He steadily increased Lafayette's field responsibilities and after a short trial period seemed comfortable viewing him as a general despite his youth. Perhaps Lafayette's age was no barrier to the commander in chief partly because of the marquis's capabilities but also because Washington himself had been named an adjutant general at age twenty in 1754 by the royal governor of Virginia and entrusted with important missions in the Appalachian wilderness.

During the first phase of Lafayette's American sojourn, which lasted about a year and a half, he participated in several engagements with the British and was wounded at the Battle of Brandywine when a musket ball passed through his left calf. Despite loss of blood and intensifying pain, he continued, as best he could, to rally the troops and postpone defeat. But defeat could not be staved off. When the retreat of the American army threatened to turn to rout, and "fugitives, cannon, and baggage crowded in complete disorder on the road to Chester," the marquis, now suffering searing pain in his calf, turned his horse at a bridge to block the passage of the troops until they had re-formed themselves into more orderly ranks. He was able to reestablish "some degree of order," he reported to Washington, who had now arrived, saw Lafayette's situation and ordered the surgeon to attend him. The following day, as Lafayette was being transferred to a boat for transport to Philadelphia, he overheard Washington instruct the surgeon, "Treat him as if he were my son."[37]

The commander in chief had no biological children of his own,[38] and more than one biographer has compared the Washington-Lafayette relationship to that of father and son. Washington had a strongly paternal relationship not only with Lafayette but with several other young men on his personal staff, most of whom served as his aides-de-camp, including John Laurens, Alexander Hamilton and Tench Tilghman, referring to them collectively as his "family." If they were all members of his family, if they were all his sons, the marquis was arguably the favorite, the bond with him exceptionally close.

Chapter 2
TURNING POINT ON THE HUDSON

Victory at Saratoga Leads to the French Alliance

The North River…a kind of key to the whole continent.
—John Adams

After Trenton, Princeton and the foraging war that followed, the events of 1777 followed a pattern reminiscent of the previous year: repeated American defeats on the battlefield followed, toward the end of the year, by a spectacular American victory, this time at Saratoga, on the Hudson River north of Albany.[39] General Burgoyne surrendered his entire British and Hessian army of seven thousand men at Saratoga to the American commander, General Gates, who had been ably assisted by Morgan's riflemen and by General Benedict Arnold (October 1777). Most of the arms used by the Americans at Saratoga had been supplied surreptitiously by France.[40] (see sidebar "Secrets and Spies" on page 72)

Both the Americans and the British attributed great strategic significance to the Hudson River. In January 1776, when General Washington was still in Massachusetts, laying siege to the British in Boston, John Adams urged him to make every effort to maintain control of New York and the Hudson River. They were the "key to the whole continent," Adams wrote in a letter to Washington, saying that no friend of the American cause could doubt "the vast importance…of that city and province [New York] and the North [Hudson] River which is in it, in the progress of this war, being the Nexus of the Northern and Southern colonies, a kind of key to the whole continent…no effort to secure it ought to be omitted."[41]

Sir Henry Clinton shared this strategic view. As early as the autumn of 1775, Clinton suggested in a letter to the duke of Newcastle that the Hudson River ought to be the primary British objective in the war.[42] In his narrative of the American campaigns, written after the war, Clinton asserted: "The River Hudson naturally presents itself as a very important object, the possession of which on the first breaking out of the disturbances might have secured to Great Britain a barrier between the southern and eastern colonies, which would have most effectually divided the strength of the inimical states."[43]

If the goal of the two sides was the same—control of the lengthy waterway—they would have to apply opposite tactics to achieve it. The British would need to plan a huge offensive operation deep in the American wilderness, far from British sources of supply at New York and on the Saint Lawrence River. The Americans' task, a defensive one, to hold the waterway on familiar ground, would not be as difficult as that faced by the British.

THREE PRONGS IN THE PLANNING, A PRONG AND A HALF IN THE EXECUTION

To achieve so important an objective, the war office in London planned a coordinated assault, combining an attack from Canada in the north with an attack from New York in the south. British plans also included a third prong, coming from the west, to create a triple pincer movement. If successful, the three prongs, converging in the Albany area, would wrest control of the Hudson-Champlain corridor from the Americans.

The three-pronged plan was never fully executed. The British did launch an attack from Canada, under General Burgoyne, but the thrust up the river from New York was delayed and, when finally attempted, too weak to be of much service to Burgoyne, who had penetrated deep into New York State, only to find himself trapped when a large American army, under General Gates, blocked his way at Saratoga. The British thrust from the west, under Lieutenant Colonel St. Leger, was attempted in a timely fashion but was thwarted at Fort Stanwix (present-day Rome, New York).

The attack from New York was postponed and feeble because the commander in chief, General William Howe, decided to emphasize an entirely different objective: he took the bulk of British and Hessian troops out of New York toward the south, conveying men and arms on a large flotilla, in order to approach the Patriot capital, Philadelphia, from the sea, disembark the troops south of the city and, from that landing point, advance on the city and capture it.

Clinton, the second in command in New York, pleaded with Howe not to abandon the master plan and, instead, dispatch British forces up the Hudson to assist Burgoyne. But Howe refused and went ahead with his movement southward (early July 1777). He instructed Clinton to remain in New York with greatly diminished troop levels.[44] Only when it was too late, Howe sent orders to Clinton to "make any diversion in favor of General Burgoyne's approaching Albany." Clinton then moved a force of moderate size up the river and was able to capture American forts some twenty miles north of New York City. It was too late to be of much help to Burgoyne, who was defeated at Saratoga and forced to surrender his huge army, consisting of 5,800 men, to Gates.[45]

Later, to explain his odd behavior, Howe said that he had not received explicit instructions from London to execute his part of the three-pronged movement. Technically, that is true. While Lord George Germain, the secretary of state for America in the war cabinet of Prime Minister Lord North, issued orders that suggested that Howe should come to Burgoyne's aid in a timely fashion, the American minister left the timing up to Howe's discretion. Howe's feeble support of Burgoyne was arguably the greatest British mistake of the war.

As we have seen, General Howe failed to seize other opportunities for the envelopment—and the likely destruction—of American armies. There were quite a few of these failures, suggesting perhaps a limited appreciation of the role of geography in war, and Howe's questionable decisions led to bitter recriminations later on.

In impressively poetic—and stinging—prose, attributed to Sir Henry Clinton, Howe's actions are described thus:

Had Sir William Howe fortified the Hills round Boston, he could not have been disgracefully driven from it: had he pursued his Victory at Long Island, he had ended the Rebellion: Had he landed above the lines at New York, not a Man could have escaped him: Had he fought the Americans at the Brunx, he was sure of Victory: had he cooperated with the N. Army, he had saved it, or had he gone to Philadelphia by land, he had ruined Mr. Washington and his Forces: But as he did none of these things, had he gone to ye D———l before he was sent to America, it had been a saving of infamy to himself and of indelible dishonour to this country.[46]

"AMERICA HAS NOW TAKEN HER RANK AMONG THE NATIONS"

Burgoyne's defeat at Saratoga in October 1777, and the surrender of nearly six thousand British and Hessian troops, stunned King George's government. The British disaster at Saratoga would soon lead to a Franco-American military alliance and would force the war office in London to alter its American strategy. Nevertheless, the king and his war ministry remained adamant. However great the setback at Saratoga, the American rebellion could still be—and must be—suppressed. If the American colonies were lost, the prestige of the British Empire would suffer an intolerable blow.[47]

Thus, the American success at Saratoga, impressive as it may have been, was not sufficient by itself to bring victory in the war. The next four years showed that French military strength, by itself, was also not enough. In order to be effective, French armed force would have to be utilized astutely. During the forty-month period that followed the Franco-American alliance and preceded the Lower Westchester Encampment, Washington repeatedly tried to strike decisive blows against the enemy with the help of French military power. None of the attempts was successful.

The victory at Saratoga had a greater impact on morale at home and on the reputation of the American army abroad than all of the American defeats of 1777. Not only morale and reputation were affected. An open American-French alliance was a direct result of Saratoga, and a treaty was signed in February 1778. The mere announcement of the treaty brought immediate benefit to the United States, for the British were compelled to divert some of their forces from the United States to protect their sugar islands in the West Indies. During a time of war, those immensely profitable islands would be at risk of French attack.

Congress was thrilled with the Franco-American treaty. It was not only a matter of military assistance. The Franco-American treaty represented international recognition, the first that the United States had ever received. Samuel Chase, a delegate to the Continental Congress from Pennsylvania, expressed the national pride: "America has now taken her rank among the nations," he said.[48]

Because of the treaty, the British decided to evacuate Philadelphia in order to consolidate their forces in New York, which would be much easier to defend from French naval attack.[49] Just before the evacuation of Philadelphia, General Howe departed for London and was replaced as British commander in chief by General Sir Henry Clinton. Soon after, Clinton evacuated Philadelphia. As British troops marched from Philadelphia across New Jersey toward New York, their rear guard was attacked by Washington's Continental army at Monmouth. Before long, the battle at Monmouth become a large scale engagement, punishing for both sides (June 28, 1778).

1778: ADMIRAL D'ESTAING'S MISSION MISCARRIES

France, now in the war officially and eager to undermine British power, provided naval aid to the Americans without delay. A few weeks after the Franco-American treaty was signed, a fleet of twelve ships of the line[50] departed Toulon, France, and set course for America under the command of Admiral d'Estaing, who was a cousin of Lafayette. The original intent in Paris was for d'Estaing to enter Delaware Bay and bottle up the British fleet at Philadelphia. Because of significant delays in crossing the Atlantic, however, the French fleet arrived in Delaware Bay after the British had evacuated the city. The enemy had escaped him.

While the first of d'Estaing's efforts had been a non-starter, the British had not gone far and, following the Battle of Monmouth, were concentrating their strength once more in New York.

The Continental army had performed impressively at Monmouth, and Washington, anticipating still greater success, quickly brought his forces into Westchester County and set up his headquarters at the Jacob Purdy House in White Plains.[51] From White Plains, he planned to strike a decisive blow against the British stronghold on Manhattan, with the help of Admiral d'Estaing's newly arrived fleet. At Washington's request, d'Estaing approached New York Harbor from the south, with the intent of initiating a coordinated naval and land attack against the enemy on Manhattan. Washington would attack from Westchester County, while d'Estaing's ships would challenge the British fleet in the waters around the city.

It was a hopeful time for the Americans. Washington perceived that the tables had been turned and that the powerful enemy had been suddenly thrown on the defensive by the new French alliance. He wrote to General Nelson:

> *It is not a little pleasing, nor less wonderful to contemplate, that after two years of maneuvering and undergoing the strangest vicissitudes, that perhaps ever attended any one contest since the creation, both armies are brought back to the very point they set out from, and that which was the offending party in the beginning is now reduced to the use of the spade and pickaxe for defense.*[52]

Washington's celebratory words were premature. To his intense frustration, the naval effort against New York, like the attempt three months before in Delaware Bay, was a non-starter: the deep draft of the French ships prevented them from crossing the bar at Sandy Hook and entering New York Harbor. Washington then proposed a third plan, the most complex of all, a joint land and sea attack against the British post at Newport, Rhode Island. The land attack would be commanded by General John Sullivan, assisted by Generals Nathanael Greene and Lafayette. D'Estaing headed east, entered Narragansett Bay and approached Newport.

Admiral Richard Howe's formidable British fleet, however, was determined to protect the British army occupying Newport. Having left New York Harbor, Howe's squadron appeared at the entrance of Narragansett Bay, forcing d'Estaing to remove his war ships from the bay and prepare for battle with Howe in the Atlantic. Before the two flotillas could engage fully, an extremely destructive storm scattered both and did such great damage to d'Estaing's ships that his naval force was rendered useless. The storm was so memorable and so violent that it was still being referred to with awe by fisherfolk in the Narragansett Bay area as the "French storm" as recently as 1945.[53]

The failure of d'Estaing's Rhode Island mission led to bitter recriminations on the part of General Sullivan, who accused the French admiral of leaving the American troops in the lurch. Sullivan recklessly made his accusations public. Because many Americans believed that Sullivan's assertions were valid, confidence in the French alliance was shaken, and the affair nearly caused a rupture in the Franco-American relationship. Washington quickly acted to repair the damage by reprimanding Sullivan for his intemperate public statements and by reassuring d'Estaing that he enjoyed Washington's complete confidence. Congress followed suit with similar reassurances, and a full-fledged crisis was averted.

Sullivan apologized for his rashness, Massachusetts governor John Hancock fêted Admiral d'Estaing day after day and Lafayette escorted the admiral on tours of Boston and the nearby towns, all the while praising America and its cause. However upset d'Estaing may have been at first, he was eventually appeased.

1778 AND 1779: AFTER THE FAILURE OF D'ESTAING'S EFFORTS—VERSAILLES RECALIBRATES AND SPAIN ENTERS THE WAR

At Versailles, there was great concern about the failure of d'Estaing's efforts. The French government concluded that the constellation of naval forces favored the British so heavily that the French navy by itself could not defeat Britain and therefore could not be decisive in the war. Great Britain and France were each increasing the sizes of their respective fleets at a rapid rate, but Britain had started with an overwhelming advantage in numbers and continued to maintain it. It would have ninety ships of the line for the 1779 campaign, whereas France would have only sixty-three. The United States had none.

It would be essential to bring the other great Bourbon power, Spain, with its fifty-eight ships of the line, into the alliance. If Spain would agree, the two Bourbon kingdoms together would outnumber the British fleet by a substantial margin.[54] Vergennes had always hoped to include the kingdom of Spain in any formal alliance with the United States. Even before Saratoga, he had courted Spain assiduously for that purpose.

Spain, however, was reluctant to join the alliance. It had no sympathy at all for the rebellious colonies in North America, let alone for the creation of republics so close to its vast possessions west of the Mississippi. The contamination of republicanism might spread! Spain refused to participate with Vergennes and Louis XVI in such a foolish alliance—at least at first.

Vergennes had felt such urgency about the American alliance in the aftermath of the American victory at Saratoga that he convinced King Louis XVI to go ahead with it even in the absence of Spanish participation. After the failed efforts of d'Estaing, however, this would no longer do. British power could not be expelled from the thirteen American states without naval supremacy, which required the addition of the Spanish fleet. Consequently, Vergennes courted Spain once more, and on the second go-around Spain consented. Like France, it feared British dominance on the seas and very much wanted to puncture British power.

The Spanish government drove a very hard bargain with Versailles. As a first stipulation, Madrid insisted that Spain would not directly ally itself with the United States, only with France. Madrid also insisted that France obligate itself to assist Spain in driving the British from the former Spanish territories of Gibraltar, Minorca and Florida. As a further stipulation, Madrid demanded that France agree to a joint invasion of England itself. Although distressed by the conditions imposed by Spain, Vergennes agreed to every one of them, and the Franco-Spanish alliance became official in April 1779.[55] As historian Jonathan Dull convincingly shows, even though Spanish participation in America's war of independence was indirect, the addition of Spain's naval power would divert enough British battleships from North America to make a critical difference to the war's outcome.[56]

More than a year later, in October 1779, d'Estaing made a fourth attempt to coordinate naval action with an American land army and cooperated with General Benjamin Lincoln in a siege of the British garrison at Savannah, Georgia. But Savannah was very well defended and could not be taken. Hundreds of American and French soldiers were killed in the attempt, and the famous Pulaski, a Polish volunteer who had volunteered his services in the American cause, also lost his life. It was extremely discouraging that another effort at coordination of French naval and American land forces had failed, and it seemed to many Americans that the French treaty, which was initially attended with so much promise, might not be able to deliver effective support in the struggle for independence.

LAFAYETTE RETURNS TO FRANCE

Lafayette, ever burning for glory, now sought new fields to conquer. He set his sights on Canada and made his case to Washington. The Americans, he argued, with the help of France should make a new attempt at its conquest.[57] Washington strongly disagreed with Lafayette's Canadian proposal but expressed his demurral gently in order to avoid insult to the irrepressible marquis.

Getting nowhere with his Canadian proposal and seeing the 1778 campaign at an end, Lafayette decided to return home. He had received a letter from his father-in-law, who assured him that Louis XVI had forgiven him for his disobedience. Coming back to France would be safe.

Lafayette broached his plans to Washington, who encouraged him to return to France. Perhaps Washington himself needed a break. Lafayette's enthusiasms, as recently exemplified by his Canadian scheme, were sometimes exhausting. Moreover, in France, the marquis might be able to obtain more French support for the American war effort. Washington recommended to Congress that Lafayette be given an indefinite leave of absence and that his rank as major general be retained. Congress and Lafayette readily agreed to this arrangement, and Congress named Lafayette liaison to the French royal court.

Lafayette returned to Paris in February 1779. The international situation had changed greatly since his departure for America almost two years before: the French-American alliance was no longer surreptitious, and the French government had, in effect, openly embraced Lafayette's American policy. Louis XVI was obligated to go through the motions of "punishing" the young marquis for his earlier disobedience, so the king ordered him confined to the mansion of his in-laws for a week. Under house arrest in lavish surroundings, he spent time with his family and was visited by countless admirers.

Immediately after this most gentle of punishments, Lafayette contacted Franklin, and the two of them got to work. The French government was eager to solicit Lafayette's advice on how to conduct the war. Lafayette obliged by preparing a report, intended for the king, with two purposes. The first was to explain the reasons for the failure of Admiral d'Estaing's mission. The other was to make recommendations on how, at this late date, when the situation seemed to be deteriorating, France could render assistance more effectively to the American rebellion.

1778–1779: London Proposes a Complicated Series of Steps to End the War

After the British defeat at Saratoga and the French-American alliance that followed, British strategic planners in London and in America had to adjust to a new and much less favorable situation. The changed circumstances eventually compelled them to adopt a "southern strategy" for the war in America. According to that strategy, the principal focus would be on "revolted provinces" in the South, where, it was felt, there was relatively strong Loyalist sentiment and relatively weak Patriot defenses. Starting from the southernmost province of Georgia and working their way north, British troops were to recover province after province for the Crown. By turning to a southern strategy, Great Britain was implicitly acknowledging that significant victories could not be expected in the northern states, at least not for a while.

Before adopting the new approach, however, the British government explored a more generous accommodation with the Americans, short of granting them independence, by sending a special delegation to America. Unlike Admiral Richard Howe's "peace" gestures in the summer of 1776, this truly represented a shift in British policy. The disaster at Saratoga had forced Crown and Parliament to put forward more favorable terms than before, and the special delegation, known as "Carlisle commissioners," was ready to offer the American states a high degree of autonomy. The First and Second Continental Congresses of 1774 and 1775 probably would have accepted the Carlisle terms. However, it was too late. The Congress of 1778, committed to the goal of full independence, would have nothing to do with the Carlisle commission. The three commissioners gave up and went home.

One of the three, William Eden, showed a keen sensitivity to what was at stake. In letters to his brother and to Alexander Wedderburn, the British attorney general, Eden's remarks still have the power to evoke deep feelings:

> "[I regret] *most heartily,*" Eden said, "*that our Rulers instead of making the Tour of Europe did not finish their education round the Coast and Rivers of the Western Side of the Atlantic...It is impossible to see what I can see of this Magnificent Country and not to go nearly mad at the long Train of Misconducts and Mistakes by which we have lost it.*"[58]

It was not at all clear to the war office that Great Britain had "lost it," and the American ministry in London was almost ready to put its new southern strategy into full gear. In fact, just before the year 1778 had expired, maneuvers in the South demonstrated that the strategy had promise when Savannah, Georgia, was seized by the forces of the Crown (December 1778). Still, the war office in London was not quite ready to abandon all infantry efforts in the North and came up with the following formula: Clinton should "endeavor without delay to bring Mr. Washington[59] to a general action"; that is, he should make one more attempt in the North to smash Washington on a battlefield in a European-style engagement, where the British would have an overwhelming advantage. Only if that endeavor "could not soon be accomplished" was Clinton "to give up every idea of offensive operation within land [in the North]...and proceed to the conquest of Georgia and the Carolinas, and make at the same time every cooperating diversion in Virginia and

Maryland, in the expectation they might lead to the entire reduction of all colonies to the southward of Susquehanna."[60]

The instructions were clear enough. Clinton put the formula into effect in late May 1779 and did so in a stepwise fashion. For the initial step, reminiscent of September and October 1777, he moved up the Hudson and fairly easily seized the two forts that protected Kings Ferry on either side of the river: Stony Point on the west, in Rockland County, and Fort Lafayette, at Verplanck on the east, in Westchester County.

The capture of the Kings Ferry forts was only the prelude. To lure Washington out of the Hudson Highlands, Clinton proceeded to rain devastation upon multiple targets in Westchester County and along the Connecticut shore, with a series of assaults that reached peak intensity in July 1779. In Westchester, the worst attacks were against Crompond, Pound Ridge and Bedford, all in the northern part of the county. The Connecticut shore attacks are described by Hufeland: "Clinton sent the notorious Tryon on [navy] vessels to the shore towns on Long Island Sound on July 3rd where in ten days they burned two hundred and forty-seven dwellings, seven churches, as well as many barns, mills, shops and vessels, mostly in Norwalk and Fairfield."

Both Clinton and Washington assumed that the British would have a decided advantage in a general engagement, and the American commander refused to be lured to his ruin.

THE STORMING OF STONY POINT

The fort and garrison…are ours. Our officers and men behaved like men who are determined to be free.
—General Anthony Wayne, describing the successful American attack at Stony Point

Through June and into July 1779, Washington resisted the temptation to confront Clinton in a large-scale battle and risk the destruction of the Continental army. Yet he conceived of another way to challenge Sir Henry's hammering attacks. Thirty months before, Washington had defeated the enemy along the Delaware River, at Trenton, by moving his army secretly and striking unexpectedly. As a result, he had won stunning victories and revived the American cause. It was time, he decided, to employ similarly clandestine tactics along the Hudson, and he ordered General Anthony "Mad Anthony" Wayne to plan a surprise for the British at Stony Point.

Donald N. Moran, military historian of the Sons of Liberty chapter of the Sons of the American Revolution, describes Wayne's attack on Stony Point, perhaps the most remarkable engagement of the war in the lower Hudson Valley:

> *General Wayne chose the recently formed light infantry brigade, consisting of 1,200 of the best soldiers in the Continental Army, for the assault…*
> *Security was extremely tight, and it has been written that local dogs were killed to prevent them from barking and alerting the British. Just before midnight on July 15th, the attacking Americans moved forward.*
>
> *To prevent an accidental firing of a musket or friendly fire incidents, the troops were ordered not to load their weapons and to only use their bayonets…*
>
> *The light infantry charged through the gaps routing the British defenders at bayonet point. The ferocity of the bayonet wielding light infantry was too much for the British defenders who surrendered.*[61]

At 2:00 a.m. on July 16, General Wayne sent this letter to General Washington: "*Dear Gen'l.* The fort and garrison with Colonel Johnston[62] are ours. Our officers and men behaved like men who are determined to be free. Yours most sincerely, Ant'y Wayne"[63]

In Sir Henry Clinton's memoirs of the war, *The American Rebellion,* it is difficult to find any words of tribute to the Continental army. His remarks about the American attack at Stony Point stand out as a rare exception: "The success attending this bold and well-combined attempt of the enemy procured very deservedly no small share of reputation and applause to the spirited officer (General Wayne) who conducted it, and was, I must confess, a very great affront to us, the more mortifying since it was unexpected and possibly avoidable."[64]

The attempt to bring Washington into a general engagement had not succeeded, and the theater of the war accordingly shifted to the south.

With Savannah, Georgia, in British hands, South Carolina became the next major target. Clinton prepared to move most of his army by sea from New York to Charleston, South Carolina, which would be put under siege. Clinton himself would command the operation, and he departed New York and sailed south with the troops in December 1779, taking his chief espionage officer, Major John Andre, with him. When Andre left for Charleston, he had been in secret communication for more than half a year with a man who claimed that he was the American general Benedict Arnold and that he wanted to be of assistance to the British side.

PARIS COMMITS A LAND ARMY TO THE AMERICAN WAR

When Lafayette, now in Paris, attempted to convince the king and Vergennes that it would be desirable to send an expeditionary land army to America to assist Washington, he was gratified to learn that they had already come to the same conclusion. True, the war was not going well, and France could not provide military assistance to the Americans indefinitely. Nevertheless, this was not the time to pull back or to reduce the level of French support. On the contrary, France would augment its military aid dramatically by sending practiced battalions to America as auxiliaries.

Lafayette then turned to the question of command. It was the marquis's feeling that the mission of Admiral d'Estaing had failed in part because of a confusing command structure, and he advised the king to make certain that the American army and the French expeditionary force operate under a unified command, with Washington as commander in chief and the French general subordinate to him. Lafayette let it be known that he hoped to be given the command of the expeditionary army himself and that he would be delighted to serve, in a subordinate capacity, under his hero, Washington. The king accepted Lafayette's recommendations regarding the command structure but did not wish to put him in charge of the mission. Instead, Louis XVI chose the Comte de Rochambeau, a battle-tested general with decades of experience, as the chief officer of the expeditionary force. According to royal instructions, which were written out and given to General Rochambeau, American officers would command French officers of equal rank, and the Comte would be subordinate to General Washington.

Having fulfilled his mission admirably as liaison from Congress, Lafayette decided that he would sail to America prior to Rochambeau's troops, prepare the Americans for the arrival of a foreign army in the United States and continue to serve in Washington's army. The king and Vergennes readily agreed.

The marquis returned to the United States in April 1780 with the astonishing and glorious news that a large French army of auxiliaries would soon follow him. Arriving in Boston, he immediately dispatched a letter to General Washington: "Here I am, my dear General, and in the midst of the joy I feel in finding myself again one of your loving

Rochambeau at Versailles.
Painter unknown.
Wikimedia Commons.

soldiers…I have affairs of the utmost importance that I should at first communicate you alone…you will easely [*sic*] know the hand of your young soldier, LAFAYETTE."[65]

Lafayette then traveled overland to Morristown, New Jersey, where Washington and the Continental army were encamped, arriving on May 10. On May 14, Washington brought James Duane up to date: "The arrival of the Marquis de Lafayette opens a prospect, which offers the most important advantages to these States…He announces an intention of his court to send a fleet and an army to cooperate effectually with us."[66]

As Lafayette had promised, the Comte de Rochambeau arrived at Newport, Rhode Island, two months later with his army and a small fleet under Admiral Ternay. The comte immediately informed Washington that he was placing himself under the American general's command. Washington would be the titular commander of both the French and American armies or, in terms that Rochambeau would sometimes use, the "generalissimo."

Admiral Ternay's flotilla consisted of eight ships of the line and two frigates.[67] For the remaining months of 1780, the flotilla stayed in Newport Harbor and saw no action, but in 1781, it would make an important contribution to the Franco-American victory at Yorktown.

Chapter 3
ROCHAMBEAU'S ARRIVAL AND ARNOLD'S TREASON

Let not an hour pass for this day must not be lost—you have news of the greatest consequence perhaps that ever happened to your country.
—Robert Townsend ("Samuel Culper Jr.")

BENEDICT ARNOLD'S TREACHERY GETS OFF TO A SLOW START

When Benedict Arnold made his initial treasonous overtures to the British in May 1779, fourteen months before Rochambeau's arrival, he found to his dismay that Sir Henry Clinton and his intelligence chief, John Andre, did not properly appreciate his value as a turncoat. Before making contact, Arnold assumed that Clinton would be more than satisfied to hear that Arnold simply wished to switch sides. That ought to have been enough. After all, Arnold, admired for his boldness and first-rate tactical sense, was one of the most capable generals in the American army. All Arnold required to close the deal was an ample monetary reward, commensurate with his well-deserved reputation. But, frustratingly, the British were not enthusiastic. They let Arnold know that merely switching sides would not be enough. At a minimum, he would have to provide worthwhile intelligence. It would be even better, they informed him, if he managed to arrange the surrender of a major rebel post. Yes, Arnold could count on a huge monetary reward, but first he would have to earn it.

Arnold attempted to comply with British demands. At first it was difficult for him to obtain valuable intelligence, however, for in 1779 he was under a cloud: Arnold had used his position as commandant at Philadelphia to engage in questionable business transactions. His dealings strongly implied conflict of interest, and Congress had initiated an investigation. Among Arnold's weaknesses was a very conspicuous love of luxury that he shared with his new wife, the pert and pretty Philadelphia Tory Peggy Shippen. She was Arnold's full partner in treason and was quite possibly its chief instigator.

Arnold's negotiations with Andre went slowly until June 1780, when he was finally able to provide intelligence of high value. By that time Arnold, who had been found guilty by Congress on some relatively minor charges and exonerated on the others, was no longer under investigation and was back in the information loop. Washington confided in him that Rochambeau's expeditionary army was soon expected to arrive in the United States and would land at Newport, Rhode Island. Arnold immediately transmitted this highly valuable intelligence to Andre and Clinton.

THE CULPER RING CALLS OUT WARNING

General Henry Clinton was naturally alarmed by the news of Rochambeau's imminent arrival and made a major effort, in July and early August 1780, to deal the French army a fatal blow by smashing it with a *coup de main*[68] at Newport before Rochambeau had a chance to set up adequate defenses. Clinton's preparations for the assault on Newport would most likely have gone undetected by Washington had not an American officer, Major Benjamin Tallmadge, already put in place an efficient spy network in New York City and on Long Island. It had been operating since 1778 and was known as the Culper Ring, a whimsical name that Washington had coined, basing it on Culpeper County, Virginia. The chief spies were Abraham Woodhull (code name "Samuel Culper") and Robert Townsend (code name "Samuel Culper Jr.").

The ring usually worked as follows: information about British military activity was uncovered by one of the "Culpers" in Manhattan, passed to an agent in Setauket, Long Island, and conveyed across Long Island Sound into Connecticut. From there it traveled from dragoon post to dragoon post until it was brought to the commander in chief himself. Drop-off points, safe houses, codes and invisible ink were all essential to the functioning of the ring. The intelligence gathered by the Culpers generally proved trustworthy and was greatly valued by Washington.

In mid-July 1780, the week that Rochambeau's army landed at Newport, Robert Townsend took note of a sudden mobilization of British troops and of transport vessels. The spy judged that the marshalling of the foe's strength was far more energetic than any he had seen before and pleaded for the Continental army to take urgent action: "The enclosed requires your immediate departure this day by all means let not an hour pass for this day must not be lost you have news of the greatest consequence perhaps that ever happened to your country."[69]

Hyperbole? Perhaps not. In truth, the danger to the French army was very great. Townsend and Woodhull informed Washington that thousands of British troops were gathering on Long Island, principally at Whitestone, which was serving as their main staging area, and that many had already embarked for the assault against Newport. It was only a few days after Rochambeau's arrival, and Rochambeau's troops, exhausted after an extremely difficult Atlantic crossing, had not had enough time to construct fortifications at Newport. The French would be highly vulnerable and almost certainly would not be able to withstand a British attack so soon after their landing. To come to their defense, Washington would have to divert Clinton, and he would have to act quickly.

Clinton also had to act quickly, however: once Rochambeau had a chance to secure his Newport base, the opportunity for a *coup de main* would be lost. As the days of July passed, many factors conspired to delay Clinton's attack, including the incompetence of British Admiral Arbuthnot and multiple crossed signals between him and Clinton. The advance notice given by Arnold was at risk of being frittered away.

Amidst the confusion and mixed signals, Clinton's informers to the north and west were reporting that Washington had started to move Continental forces across Westchester toward Manhattan. The British commander recognized that the rebel army's movement might be a feint. But it might also represent an impending attack on his skeleton force remaining in New York City. A cautious tactician, Clinton could not accept the growing risk to his depleted New York garrison. Already frustrated by the long delays caused by the bungling admiral, and unnerved by the menace threatening him from Westchester, Clinton decided that he would not weaken his defenses in New York any longer. The attack on Rochambeau's army was given up.

As Clinton returned his forces to New York, Washington withdrew the Continental army from Westchester. The British fleet kept on the prowl east of Long Island, bottling up the French flotilla in Narragansett Bay. Nevertheless, by early August, the window of opportunity had closed: the British had squandered their chance to wreck the Franco-American alliance, and Robert Townsend and Abraham Woodhull had rendered inestimable service to their country.

When Clinton pulled back from his Newport operation, Arnold was offering him an even greater prize: the Hudson River stronghold at West Point. In July, Arnold had convinced Washington to put him in charge of the post. He became commander there on August 2 and was offering to sell it (and the two thousand American troops defending it) to Clinton for £20,000. Why worry about Rochambeau's army, whose defenses at Newport were, in any case, strengthening by the day when the fortifications of West Point were about to fall effortlessly into British hands?

What was the significance of West Point? Stalemate persisted in the war, it could be argued, because neither side dominated the Hudson–Lake Champlain corridor. The British held the northern and southern anchors at Quebec and at New York. In between those two anchors, the Americans, for the most part, controlled the length of waterway. As long as the Americans did, large bodies of Continental troops—even entire armies—plus war supplies and communication and commerce of all kinds could pass back and forth between the four New England states to the east and the nine states to the west and south.

If control of West Point were to pass to the Crown, however, the Americans would lose strategic domination of the waterway, for the fortifications established at West Point by 1780 had significantly

View of West Point from above Washington Valley, about 1870. Unidentified artist, American, nineteenth century. *Photograph © 2011 Museum of Fine Arts, Boston.*

supplemented its natural geographic advantages. If Great Britain could seize the citadel, and if Britain's huge naval advantages were added to the mix, the king's ships would be able to patrol the length of the water corridor, effectively establishing control, and the Americans would no longer be able to move significant supplies across, let alone battalions or armies. In John Adams's apt phrase, the Hudson was the "key to the continent." By 1780, West Point had become the place where the British could turn the key, gain ascendancy on the river and secure the continent, dealing a deathblow to the rebellion.

Rochambeau Settles in at Newport

The appearance of Rochambeau's expeditionary force at Newport seemed like a godsend to the struggling Continental army and generated a burst of enthusiasm in the American camps on the west side of the

Hudson. Washington ordered the creation of a black-and-white cockade to be worn by Continental troops, representing the alliance of the United States and France, and he sent the following greeting to Rochambeau: "I hasten to communicate to you with what happiness I have received the auspicious news of your safe arrival, and in my name and in the name of the American Army I present to you the assurance of my deep appreciation and my lively gratitude to the Allies who have come so generously to our aid."[70]

Rochambeau very quickly received bad news about the state of the American military, however: the French consul in Boston informed him that Washington "had with him only a handful of men, and that their morale [is] very low."[71]

The French ambassador to the United States, M. Luzerne, could not deny that Washington had insufficient troops, but he hastened to reassure General Rochambeau that the consul's assertions about American morale were incorrect: "There is an excellent spirit in the American army," Luzerne insisted. "The Continental soldier is inured to fatigue, and their officers are yearning to distinguish themselves."[72] While the state of morale in the American army was not entirely clear in the summer of 1780, and a case could perhaps be made on either side, events of the next fifteen months would confirm that it was the ambassador, and not the consul, who was right.

Whatever might be the case regarding the morale of the American soldier, his numbers were, without question, too few. Congress had no power to recruit troops, and Washington had to make his appeal to the individual states. He wrote to Lafayette:

> *The die is cast, and it remains with the states to fulfill their engagements, to preserve their credit, and support their independence or involve us in disgrace and defeat...I shall proceed on the supposition that they will ultimately consult their own interest and honor and not suffer us to fail for want of means which it is evidently in their power to afford.*[73]

Nor was the problem merely one of numbers of troops. Continental currency had depreciated greatly during the war, making it nearly impossible by the year 1780 to purchase military supplies with Continental dollars.[74] The depreciation of the currency has long been attributed to excessive printing of paper money by the Congress. But there was an additional reason for the decline in value of American currency, a campaign on the part of the British in New York to undermine the American economy by producing reams of bogus Continental bills. The Culper Ring discovered how massive the campaign was. The order to turn out the bogus bills came from the British high command itself, in the person of George Germain. At one point, General William Tryon, commander of the Loyalists in New York, was directly in charge of one of the counterfeiting workshops. After the counterfeit bills were produced, it was essential to get them into the American countryside. This was done by publishing newspaper advertisements offering free money, "any number of counterfeit Congress-notes," to "persons going into the other colonies." When Washington was shown the ad, he angrily wrote to Congress that it demonstrated "that no artifices are left untried by the enemy to injure us."[75]

The currency collapse forced Congress, on March 18, 1780, to recall all of its bills in circulation.[76] Rochambeau addressed the economic crisis in his first report to Vergennes by indicating that the value of Continental paper money had fallen to sixty for one. Rochambeau added: "The war will be an expensive one. We pay even for our quarters and the land occupied by the camp. I shall, of course, use all possible order and economy. Send us troops and money, but do not depend upon these people or upon their means. They have neither money nor credit."[77]

CONTRETEMPS BETWEEN ROCHAMBEAU AND LAFAYETTE

Naval superiority, Rochambeau and Washington agreed, would be essential for victory. The flotilla at Newport was too small to achieve superiority at sea and, in any case, was hemmed in by the British navy, lying in wait east of Long Island Sound. In his messages from Rhode Island to Versailles, Rochambeau made appeals again and again for more French warships: "We must have naval superiority—that is indispensable for the success of the campaign."[78]

On this very issue, Lafayette's impetuosity got a bit out of control and led to a contretemps with Rochambeau. Their disagreement illustrates the high premium that Rochambeau placed on naval supremacy.

"Lafayette…sends me a letter of 12 pages…he now proposes such extravagant things as taking Long Island and New York without the assistance of the Navy!" Rochambeau wrote in exasperation to Ambassador Luzerne on August 14, 1780.

Luzerne wrote back to Rochambeau: "What Lafayette has written to you is purely the result of zeal and of a high courage which experience will moderate."[79]

Thoroughly chastened, Lafayette applied all of his charm to mend the fractured relationship with the older general. "If I have offended you," he wrote to Rochambeau on August 16, "I apologize for two reasons, the first because I love you, and the second because my intention here is to do everything to please you…I would make every sacrifice…to contribute to [French] glory, to their comfort, to their union with the Americans."[80]

On August 27, Rochambeau gave this answer to the marquis:

It is always well to think the French invincible, my dear Marquis, but let me tell you a great secret which I have learnt from 40 years service with them. There are no troops more easily beaten when they have lost confidence in their leaders, and they lose this confidence immediately when they see that they are called upon to suffer because of an individual ambition…Please be assured of my warmest friendship, and if I have brought to your attention the things which displeased me in your last letter, it was because I had concluded that the warmth of your heart and of your soul had for the moment gotten the better of your wisdom and judgment. Retain this last quality for the council chamber and reserve all of the first spirit for the moment when plans are to be put into execution.[81]

Meeting at Hartford; Arnold Reappears on the Stage

The first Washington-Rochambeau meeting, which took place in late September at Hartford, is memorable not because of the decisions taken there but because of its close association with Benedict Arnold's treachery. Both before the meeting and after it, Arnold stepped onto the stage to play out his unique role as "the most senior mole in espionage history."[82]

Arnold's performance now became personal and vile: he informed Andre in New York that Washington, who had been Arnold's constant supporter and admirer, would be crossing the Hudson River at Kings Ferry with a small entourage on his way to Hartford on September 18. This would be a perfect occasion to seize or kill the American commander in chief. Washington had written to Arnold, "I want to make my journey a secret." Arnold wrote to Andre, "General Washington will be at Kings Ferry Sunday evening next on his way to Hartford where he is to meet the French admiral and general. And will lodge at Peek's Kill."[83] Arnold's letter would surely have done the trick, but it arrived at headquarters in New York one day late. Another missed opportunity. No matter! While Washington conferred with the French in Hartford, Arnold was preparing West Point for its transfer to the British.

The Hartford session itself was a disappointment, for it revealed the hard truth to Washington that Rochambeau did not have sufficient numbers of men to have a decisive impact in any attack on Clinton's well-defended army on Manhattan. The meeting was equally disappointing to Rochambeau, who heard firsthand from Washington that the American battalions were grossly undermanned. All Washington could do was plead with the various states to meet the recruitment quotas that had been set by Congress. The bitterest disappointment, for Washington and Rochambeau both, was the news that a French fleet under Admiral Guichen, a naval presence they had been counting on, would be heading for the West Indies instead of New York.

SEPTEMBER 1780: MAJOR ANDRE AND BENEDICT ARNOLD

Sir Henry was naturally eager to acquire West Point at the earliest possible date, and his foremost efforts were now directed toward negotiations with Benedict Arnold. Major Andre continued to serve as the principal go-between. In general, when representatives from the warring parties wished to discuss matters of mutual interest, they often found it convenient to parlay at a location on the front lines under flags of truce. Dobbs Ferry, as the southernmost American guard post on the Hudson River in September 1780, was, in effect, situated on the front lines,[84] and Andre and Arnold attempted to have their parlay there.

Andre, who had adopted the bogus name of John Anderson, prepared for the meeting by writing the following disingenuous letter to Colonel Elisha Sheldon, who was stationed in northern Westchester. As commander of an American dragoon detachment in Westchester County, Sheldon had authority over the forward guard post at Dobbs Ferry. "John Anderson" wrote:

> *I hope* [for] *your indulgence in permitting me to meet a friend near your outposts. I will endeavor to obtain permission to go out with a flag, which will be sent to Dobbs's Ferry on Monday next, the 11th instant* [September 11, 1780], *at twelve o'clock…Let me entreat you, sir, to favor a matter so interesting to the parties concerned, and which is of so private a nature that the public on neither side can be injured by it.*

Andre, traveling from New York by land, arrived at Dobbs Ferry on September 11. On that same day, Arnold tried to come to Dobbs Ferry by barge but failed to reach shore, for as he approached the landing site, his barge was driven off by fire from a British gunboat. Sir Henry Clinton, who wanted this meeting badly, had neglected to communicate hold-your-fire orders to British vessels on the river. As a consequence, the Dobbs Ferry meeting did not take place.

Both parties remained deeply interested, of course, in so important an object as the transfer of West Point into British hands (as well as the transfer of a large purse into Arnold's hands), and nine days later a meeting between Andre and Arnold did take place about fifteen miles north of Dobbs Ferry, on the opposite shore, near Haverstraw. This time Major Andre traveled by water to the meeting place on the British warship *Vulcan*.

Through the night in a cove by the Hudson shore, Andre and Arnold worked out the terms of their transaction. At dawn, with the negotiations satisfactorily concluded, Arnold presented Andre with several papers detailing the best means to capture West Point. These invaluable documents guaranteed the capture of the garrison. All Andre had to do was get the papers back to Sir Henry in New York. Once in the hands of the British commander, the rest would be easy, the securing of West Point a certainty.

However, Major Andre was suddenly faced with a major problem. The *Vulcan*, which had expeditiously brought the major to the meeting place, was now gone. It had been driven off by American artillery on the eastern (Westchester) shore and was no longer available to bring him back to New York.

Andre was not on the front lines but was deep within American-held territory. He would have to find his way back to New York by crossing to the east side of the Hudson at Kings Ferry and then by traveling overland through Westchester County, past several American posts.

Arnold had the answer. First, he would provide Andre with a note, instructing American troops to permit the bearer, John Anderson, to pass unhindered. The general then advised the major to remove his uniform and don civilian garb instead. After all, how could Andre expect to travel unchallenged past American checkpoints while wearing the uniform of the enemy? Andre was extremely reluctant to do this; removing his uniform and dressing as a civilian, while carrying the West Point documents, would force him to play the odious role of a spy. If he were captured, he would therefore be dealt with as a spy and could not expect the privileges accorded to a prisoner of war. There appeared to be little choice, however, and Andre changed into civilian clothes.

Andre Attempts to Return to New York

Arnold suggested that Andre hide the precious papers between his sock and foot and provided him with an escort, who proved quite useful to the British major at first, accompanying him across Kings Ferry and helping him talk his way past American checkpoints in Westchester County. The escort was willing to be helpful only so far, however, and accompanied Andre only part of the way. A little south of the Croton River, the escort turned back, and Andre was on his own. At the final checkpoint, an American guard warned Andre to keep to the interior of the county as he traveled south, advising him to proceed through White Plains, for there were many British patrols, the American guard said, closer to the river.

That was all that Andre needed to hear. He headed west on horseback toward the river, hoping that he would quickly run into a British or a Loyalist patrol. Near Tarrytown when he was stopped by three armed men, he let his hopes overrule his judgment, and he gave the game away by expressing the wish that the three men were of "the lower party."

Fortunately for the United States, they were not. Deeply suspicious of the nervous horseman, they ordered him to dismount and did a thorough search, finding the incriminating papers in his sock. The militiamen immediately understood that they had captured a spy, and a short time later, Washington himself would have the papers in his hand. Arnold, however, also learned quickly that his betrayal had been exposed; just hours before Washington ordered his arrest, the traitor was able to escape to New York.[85]

The three men whose suspicions had saved the country were John Paulding, Isaac Van Wart and David Williams, Westchester militiamen, and part of a larger unit of seven stationed near Bedford.[86] All seven were on a mission that morning and had ridden south to intercept Cow-Boy raiders in the Tarrytown area. The other four members of the unit were positioned nearby, ready to come to the assistance of the Paulding group in case of trouble. The leader of the militia unit was John Dean, whose instructions came from Lieutenant Colonel John Jameson, an officer in Colonel Sheldon's dragoons.

Major Andre was tried as a spy by a military court, sentenced to death and hanged on October 2, 1780, at Tappan, in Rockland County, nine days after his capture in Tarrytown.

John Champe

Having safely arrived in New York, Benedict Arnold was given a substantial monetary reward by Sir Henry Clinton and commissioned a brigadier general in the British army. Arnold promptly announced that he was raising a corps of cavalry and infantry to fight on the side of the Crown. This, he said, would be "a Chosen Band of Americans… to share in the glory of rescuing our native country from the grasping hand of France."[87]

Arnold had limited success in raising his regiment. But a few did join the "Chosen Band." Among them was a huge and powerful man by the name of John Champe. Unlike Arnold's other troops, Champe was simultaneously a loyal soldier in Washington's army, a highly regarded sergeant major in the cavalry unit of Major Light Horse Harry Lee.[88] Lee had sent Champe to New York to kidnap Arnold and bring him back alive to Washington.

It had not been easy to convince Champe to accept the mission. He was told that he would have to fake a desertion from the American army and flee to New York. Once there, assisted by a single confederate, he would have to overpower Arnold, tie him up and spirit him across the Hudson to Major Lee's New Jersey camp. Champe was finally won over by the obvious importance of the assignment and the promise of full honors and a lieutenant's commission upon delivery of the hated traitor to the commander in chief. Washington had ordered the kidnapping, which he acknowledged was a "delicate and hazardous project." But he also called it "indispensable."[89]

Champe's career as kidnapper did indeed prove hazardous, and it is remarkable that he survived it. What is perhaps even more remarkable is that he came close to succeeding at his mission. In New York, Champe won Arnold's confidence and joined his "Chosen Band." Taking great risks, he cased Arnold's house and studied his quarry's habits. Champe noted that Arnold regularly availed himself of the outhouse late at night. This would be the ideal place and time to capture him, preferably on a moonless night, in deep darkness. Champe went so far as to loosen several slats in the fence surrounding Arnold's yard so that the captive could more easily be dragged away. The sergeant major went over the details with his confederate and arranged for a boatman to carry the two kidnappers, with Arnold well in hand, across the Hudson. Word was passed to Major Lee in New Jersey, and a date was chosen for the abduction, December 11. Lee would be waiting for the captive on the Jersey shore.

The kidnapping attempt was foiled at the eleventh hour by a completely unexpected decision on Arnold's part. He had begun to fear that the recruits of his regiment, deserters all, would desert again. To forestall that possibility, he ordered the recruits, including Champe, to board a transport vessel in the harbor.

Except for Arnold's last-minute decision, Champe might actually have carried off the mission, for he had planned it meticulously. Instead, he found himself trapped on a British troop ship in New York Harbor. There he would stay for three weeks. He finally debarked around New Year's Day 1781 in Virginia, as part of an army of 1,600 Loyalist, British and Hessian troops under Arnold's command.

Arnold entered Virginia with a vengeance and proceeded to despoil the state, plundering tobacco crops and grain warehouses, destroying other properties and spreading devastation in the James River Valley. Champe, a Virginian, had hoped to return to his native state a hero. But now, as an unwilling soldier in Arnold's army, he found himself one of its pillagers instead.[90]

In the North, New Year's Day 1781 brought what was potentially an even more ominous development: the mutiny of a critical component of the Continental army, the 1,300 men of the Pennsylvania line. It was the beginning of a tumultuous year for the United States.

SECRETS AND SPIES

While the open war was raging, behind the scenes there was a secret war, essential for bringing military supplies from Europe to the Patriot forces. In the early months of the rebellion, the Continental army found it extremely difficult to obtain ammunition. In July 1775, the month that Washington assumed command, he reported to Congress: "We are so exceedingly destitute that our artillery will be of little use, without a supply both large and seasonable. What we have must be reserved for the small arms, and that managed with the utmost frugality."[91] And on Christmas Day 1775, he told Congress: "Our want of powder is inconceivable."[92]

The Americans had a miniscule manufacturing capability, could not furnish themselves with adequate ordnance and were utterly dependent on European sources. Without the supply that came from abroad, the rebellion would have fizzled to nothing. That is why massive gunrunning enterprises were such an important aspect of the secret war. Gun merchants in the Dutch Republic, France, Spain and even England were involved. In some cases, they shipped directly to American ports, but it was generally safer to disguise the operations by using intermediate stations in the Caribbean. The Leeward Islands in the West Indies, most notably the Dutch island of Eustacia (known to the Americans as "Stacia") and the French island of Martinique, became veritable ammunition warehouses, servicing the needs of the American uprising.

Gunrunning to the colonies had begun even before the Battles of Lexington and Concord. The British ambassador in the Hague, Mr. Yorke, was well aware that ammunition was being conveyed to the rebels on vessels coming from Holland and reported the danger to London. The British navy could not risk war by entering Dutch ports. The best that they could do was attempt to intercept the arms-bearing vessels once they entered international waters. The captains of the vessels were exceedingly wily, however: while some of them were caught, most got through.

The secret war was organized by highly placed government officials and by some of the most prominent personalities of the age, including Benjamin Franklin and the French playwright Beaumarchais, author of the *Barber of Seville* and the *Marriage of Figaro*. In 1776, Silas Deane worked closely with Beaumarchais to set up a large-scale smuggling enterprise, focusing on military ordnance of all kinds. Beaumarchais, in turn, worked closely with French foreign minister, Charles Vergennes, and suggested to him that a dummy commercial company be created to provide cover for the gunrunners. Vergennes agreed and arranged to back up the operation with a large infusion of funds from the French treasury. The dummy commercial firm was given the Spanish name Roderigue Hortalez et Cie. When Benjamin Franklin arrived in Paris to join Silas Deane as emissary to the court of Louis XVI, he quickly understood that the actual name of Hortalez et Cie. was France.

In April 1777, an enormous supply of ordnance was brought to Portsmouth, New Hampshire, by Hortalez et Cie. Most of the ammunition that was used at the Battle of Saratoga was drawn from that supply.[93] Would the Americans have won the Battle of Saratoga without that arms shipment? It is difficult to see how. While many factors contributed to the victory at Saratoga, an indispensable contribution was made by Hortalez et Cie.—France!

Espionage was another central aspect of the secret war and played an outsized role in the struggle for independence. The most successful long-term American spies were probably Robert Townsend and Abraham Woodhull of the Culper Ring, whose contributions are described in the text. Perhaps the most successful long-term British spy was Edward Bancroft, first secretary to Benjamin Franklin in Paris. Bancroft had access to the most important documents that passed across Franklin's desk, and on a weekly schedule he reported what was going on to his handlers, British agents in Paris.

Bancroft was a very personable gentleman, and Franklin was drawn to him largely because he was a fellow scientist of some achievement, an expert in tropical plants. The two had met before the war in London, and Bancroft enjoyed the American emissary's full confidence. Sixty years later, documents found in British governmental archives gave proof of Bancroft's spying.

Chapter 4

Episodes from the War in Westchester

Prelude

August 1774: Philipsburg and White Plains

Frederick Philipse III, the lord of the manor of Philipsburg, was a mild-mannered man with conservative inclinations, and he was sometimes asked by other Westchester men of means to accept leadership positions in the county in the years before the war.[94] So it was not surprising that he was elected chairman of a special "county convention" that met in White Plains on August 22, 1774.

The county convention on August 22 was the first of its kind, and the conservative leaders of the county really didn't want it.[95] They accepted it because New York City's committee of correspondence had called for it and because public sentiment seemed to favor it. The conservatives reasoned that the county convention would, in any case, not be very dangerous, since they had the political clout to dominate the proceedings.

Philipse and his allies were not sympathetic to the idea of a special county convention for one simple reason: however tame its actions, the convention would be a rebuke directed against Parliament, which had just enacted draconian legislation to punish Boston and Massachusetts for the Boston Tea Party of December 16, 1773. The Parliamentary legislation, called the Coercive Acts (and reviled in America as the "Intolerable Acts"), had shut down the port of Boston and abolished self-government in Massachusetts.

The Westchester conservatives notwithstanding, many other Americans were outspoken in their criticism of Parliament. In New York, as in the other colonies, the Coercive Acts were widely viewed as an expression of contempt for colonial self-government. A Parliament willing to abolish popularly elected legislative bodies in Massachusetts would be willing to abolish them in New York and in every other colony.

The Coercive Acts sparked a political crisis in North America. By 1774 the people of the thirteen colonies—those who were free—had known six generations of self-rule. They were probably the most politically attuned people on the face of the earth, and they dealt with the crisis in a politically sagacious way: by creating a legislative body to represent all of the colonies, a Continental Congress, which would meet in Philadelphia in September 1774.[96]

New York City's committee of correspondence had sent circulars to the leaders of all the counties of the province of New York, asking them to meet in county conventions, approve members of the committee of correspondence to serve as the New York delegates to the Philadelphia congress or suggest delegates of their own.

At the county convention on August 22, which met at the White Plains courthouse, harmony reigned, or so it seemed. Philipse and his conservative allies accepted the concept of a Continental Congress. No doubt they did so in order to discourage dissent at the convention and mollify public opinion. It seemed to be a good tactic at the time. But if they had foreseen the role that the Philadelphia congress would play, they would have thought twice.

1774 AND 1775: THE FIRST CONTINENTAL CONGRESS AND THE WAR OF THE PAMPHLETS

The Philadelphia congress met in September and October 1774 and called itself the "Congress of the United Colonies of America." Before long it became known as the First Continental Congress. The delegates to the Congress attempted to achieve a difficult balance, emphasizing moderation and firmness at the same time. The former is evident in their petition to the King: "We wish not…the grant of any new right. Your royal authority over us, and our connection with Great Britain we shall always support and maintain."[97]

For an expression of firmness, the Congress turned to one of its most eloquent delegates, John Jay, a Westchester lawyer from Rye, asking him to write an Address to the People of Great Britain: "But if you are determined that your ministers shall wantonly sport with the rights of mankind…we must then tell you that we will never submit to be the hewers of wood or drawers of water, for any ministry or nation in the world."[98]

They were strong words of defiance, and the delegates backed them up with strong action, passing a nonimportation act, which called for a boycott of all British goods, and creating associations in each colony to enforce the boycott.

This was real retaliation, and for Philipse and his allies in Westchester County, it was a step much too far. By the spring of 1775, when a call was issued to assemble again in White Plains to choose delegates for a second Continental Congress, all could see that the previous harmony had fallen apart and had been replaced by angry division.

When the political men of the county met on April 11, 1775, once more at the White Plains courthouse, the Philipse faction looked over the persons gathered, counted the votes in their heads and recognized that they would be in the minority. This they refused to accept and walked out of the courthouse, calling the assembly there "illegal." Meeting at a different location in White Plains as a rival group, they issued a statement condemning "all unlawful congresses": "We the subscribers, Freeholders and Inhabitants of the County of Westchester having assembled at White Plains…do declare our honest abhorrence of all unlawful congresses and committees, and that we are determined at the hazard of our lives and properties, to support [the] King."

Westchester County and New York were entering a period in their political history called "the war of the pamphlets." It was a war of invective, waged in print in the months prior to Lexington and Concord by articulate political adversaries. The most notable were Samuel Seabury, an Anglican rector, Tory and nimble polemicist, who wrote

Alexander Hamilton, 1806. John Trumbull. *Photograph © 2011 Museum of Fine Arts, Boston.*

under the pen name "A Westchester Farmer," and Alexander Hamilton, a precocious student and committed Whig at King's College.[99]

In *An Alarm to the Legislature of the Province of New-York*, Seabury condemned the effrontery of those who dared to defy the British nation and its government: "Nothing seems to be consulted, but how to perplex, irritate, and affront, the British Ministry, Parliament, Nation and King...nothing is called FREEDOM but SEDITION! Nothing LIBERTY but REBELLION!"[100]

In *The Farmer Refuted*, Hamilton replied:

> *If we examine the pretensions of parliament...we shall, presently detect their injustice. First, they are subversive of our natural liberty, because an authority is assumed over us, which we by no means assent to...*
>
> *And secondly, they divest us of that moral security, for our lives and properties, which we are intitled [sic] to, and which it is the primary end of society to bestow. For such security can never exist, while we have no part in making the laws, that are to bind us...the sacred rights of mankind are not to be rummaged for among old parchments or musty*

papers. They are written, as with a sunbeam, in the whole volume of human nature by the hand of the divinity itself and can never be erased or obscured by mortal power.[101]

1776: THE UPPER AND LOWER PARTIES AND THE "NEUTRAL GROUND" BETWEEN THEM

Soon after the huge British expeditionary force, under the command of General William Howe and his brother, Admiral Richard Howe, arrived in New York Harbor in the summer of 1776, the British commanders sent two warships, the *Phoenix* and the *Rose*, up the Hudson into the wide river expanse that is known as the Tappan Zee. The ships remained in the Hudson for several weeks, positioning themselves in the middle of the Tappan Zee, where they were out of range of American cannon fire. This penetration of the Hudson mattered tactically because captains and crews were able to communicate with Loyalists on shore, supply them with weapons and collaborate with them on strategies to undermine local Patriot forces.[102]

While the British dominated the river, the Americans in Westchester contested control on land and were able to establish a relatively safe zone in the Hudson Highlands, north of the Croton River. Soon after the battle of White Plains, Washington established American headquarters for the Hudson Highlands at Peekskill. After West Point was garrisoned early in 1778, headquarters for the Highlands were transferred there, but the front lines for the American army remained at or near Peekskill and encompassed fortifications a few miles south of Peekskill at Verplanck and across the river on the western shore at Stony Point, two posts that served to protect the Hudson River crossing at Kings Ferry. At times of relative security, the Americans attempted to maintain their advance posts as far south as Dobbs Ferry, since that Hudson crossing point allowed relatively speedy communication between New England and the southern states.

Following their capture of Fort Washington and Fort Lee in November 1776, the British established a northern perimeter for Manhattan at Kingsbridge. This line was attacked on several occasions but was not successfully breached at any time during the war. While the American perimeter in the Peekskill area was occasionally breached, the American and British lines took on a semi-permanent character and so defined the territories of the "Upper Party" and the "Lower Party" in Westchester for much of the war. The "neutral ground" referred to territory that lay between the American and British lines. Its boundaries were not sharply delineated but instead shifted as dominance seesawed back and forth between the contending sides.

1777: ASCENDANT AT FIRST, THE BRITISH RETRENCH AFTER THEIR DEFEAT AT SARATOGA

In the lower Hudson Valley, changes in military ascendancy reflected developments in the broader war. British predominance was established after General William Howe's victory at the Battle of White Plains (October 1776) and continued until General John Burgoyne's defeat at Saratoga twelve months later. British power during this period was most dramatically manifested in September and October 1777, when Sir Henry Clinton launched an attack up the Hudson, pushing aside weak American opposition and capturing one post after another in the lower Hudson Valley, first at Stony Point and then at Fort Montgomery and Fort Clinton (named for the American commander James Clinton). He seized those forts as part of a tardy and ultimately unsuccessful effort to aid General Burgoyne, beleaguered at Saratoga, 125 miles to the north, so Clinton's moves up the Hudson represented a British failure on the broader scale. Nevertheless, the seizure of the forts meant true British ascendancy in the Westchester County region. British victories in the lower Hudson Valley gave cover for Loyalist surrogates of the Crown, such as Simcoe's Queen's Rangers and Delancey's Refugees, to take a relatively free hand by attacking Patriot households and farms, foraging widely and stealing cattle throughout Westchester (hence the term "Cow-boys"). The November 1777 attack on the homes of the Van Tassels at Storm's Bridge and the brutal beating of Vincent, Lawrence and Smith on the Dobbs Ferry Road occurred during this period.

Dominance in the lower Hudson quickly shifted, however, after the British defeat at Saratoga. The British were staggered by Saratoga and by the French-American alliance that followed. In response, they retrenched. Withdrawing into their Manhattan Island fortress, they remained on defense for almost a year. In November and December 1777, as the first step in the new defensive posture, Clinton was ordered by Howe, now ensconced in Philadelphia, to pull back from the lower Hudson forts that he had just captured. Howe's orders appalled Clinton. He considered them foolish in the extreme, another example of the ineptitude of the commander in chief. Why pull back from advantageous positions in a region as strategically significant as the Hudson Valley? But Clinton had no choice in the matter. Depressed by the turn of events, and furious at Howe, he pulled back from his hard-won conquests.

1778: Ascendancy in the Region Shifts Once More—Valentine's Hill and Edgar's Lane

By the late summer, ascendancy in the lower Hudson region was seesawing back to the Crown and to its Loyalist and Hessian auxiliaries, who did not wait long to show that they had regained the initiative.[103] The British cavalry leader, Banastre Tarleton, infamous two years later at Waxhaws, South Carolina, for murdering hundreds of surrendering American soldiers who were pleading for quarter ("Bloody Tarleton," "Bloody Ban" and "Tarleton's quarters" became well-known phrases), joined forces on August 31, 1778, with Lieutenant Colonel Simcoe's Queen's Rangers for an attack on an American outpost commanded by Colonel Gist near Valentine's Hill (in the southeastern section of Yonkers today). A company of Stockbridge Indians, allies of the Patriots, constituted an advance American guard and were posted a short distance to the south, near the present-day Bronx boundary.[104] Historian Otto Hufeland relates that the outnumbered Indians fled from Tarleton's dragoons, who pursued them over open fields and killed most of them. Of the fifty Indians, only two were taken prisoner.[105]

This brutal action occurred only twenty miles south of the Continental army, still deployed in White Plains. The proximity of Washington's twenty-three thousand American troops may have given Tarleton and Simcoe pause about venturing farther north. But the Continental army soon departed from White Plains. On September 16, the American commander redeployed his army in Fredericksburg (now called Patterson, in present-day Putnam County).[106]

Two weeks after Washington's withdrawal from White Plains, a Hessian patrol of eighty men, including about sixteen mounted troops (Jaegers), entered present-day Hastings along the river road (Broadway today), in the area of Edgar's Lane. The patrol was commanded by Captain von Donop and was based near Kingsbridge. At Peter Post's farm in the northern part of Hastings, they encountered Mr. Post and asked him if any rebels were about. Post, it appears, was aware that American dragoons were lying in wait for the Hessians and directed them into the ambush. The Hessian company was routed by the Americans, who were commanded by Colonel Elisha Sheldon and Major Light Horse Harry Lee. The Hessian survivors scurried back to Kingsbridge, where they plotted their revenge on Peter Post. When the American defenders were gone, the Jaegers returned to his farm and, as Hufeland recounts, "beat him until he was left for dead." But Peter Post survived. He recovered from the beating and continued to live in Hastings for many years.[107]

1779: The Most Intense Attacks of the War

In the summer of 1779, Clinton launched intense attacks against communities in Westchester and along the Connecticut coast, trying (as mentioned in Chapter 2) to tempt Washington out of his well-defended cantonments in the Hudson Highlands and draw him into a general engagement.[108] As we examine the Westchester raids of 1779, the name of Banastre Tarleton is prominent again. In the first week of July, Tarleton's cavalry struck in the northern part of the county and tried to surprise the American dragoons at Pound Ridge, hoping to capture its commander, Colonel Sheldon. Popularly known as "Sheldon's Horse" and "Washington's Eyes," Sheldon's dragoons were composed of Connecticut men. They had been commissioned by Congress in December 1776 at the recommendation of General Washington and, in 1779, were serving as the principal mounted troops in the county. Luckily, Sheldon had some forewarning of Tarleton's attack: a spy by the name of Luther Kinnicutt knew that a raid was planned. Regrettably, he did not know the date. Nevertheless, because of Kinnicutt's information, imprecise as it was, Sheldon was able to take the precaution of keeping his horses saddled. But Tarleton was clever enough to attack at night during a rainstorm, when Sheldon felt an attack was unlikely. Between two hundred and three hundred British horsemen left their base at Mile Square (in southeast Yonkers today) late that stormy night and were in northern Westchester by 4:00 a.m. on July 2.[109]

Sheldon then had another stroke of luck: Tarleton's dragoons took a wrong turn. Before they discovered their error, they themselves had been discovered by a small body of sentinels led by Benjamin Tallmadge, who galloped back to arouse the rest of Sheldon's men. The American dragoons had time to mount their horses, but barely. They hastened away with Tarleton in close pursuit. A skirmish ensued, and the Americans had the worst of it: ten were wounded and eight taken prisoner.[110]

Despite the technical victory, the episode was apparently a frustrating one for Tarleton. Most of the American dragoons, including their leader, Sheldon, had escaped him. Tarleton's subsequent actions that morning would seem to attest to his frustration. His dragoons turned back to Pound Ridge where they burned the Presbyterian church and went about plundering the place. Tarleton's men then entered nearby Bedford, where several citizens fired at them from their houses. In response, Tarleton proceeded to burn the town down. According to Shonnard and Spooner, "The ancient settlement of Bedford was practically swept out of existence."[111]

THE SOUTHERN STRATEGY AND ITS EFFECT ON WESTCHESTER

Britain's southern strategy had a significant impact on the war in Westchester County. Because a large portion of Sir Henry's army was abruptly detached for service in the South, the Hudson River region, at the close of 1779, started to enjoy a bit of relief. Clinton left New York with the troop detachment in December 1779, sailing to South Carolina, and Hessian General Knyphausen was left in charge in Manhattan.

Regrettably, with Knyphausen in charge, Westchester experienced only a measure of relief. Yes, compared with the intense raids of the summer of 1779, compared with the burning of whole towns, the situation was improved. Knyphausen, though, was an aggressive commander. Low troop levels notwithstanding, he acted with determination and didn't hesitate to launch targeted attacks. The largest and most successful was the raid on Joseph Youngs's house and tavern in February 1780.

YOUNGS CORNERS

Youngs, an activist and militiaman, was, at fifty-eight, older than most of the other politically involved and active Patriots. His property was situated at a central Westchester crossroads known as Four Corners (or Youngs Corners), on high ground about four miles inland from the Hudson River. Today the locality is the site of Blythedale Children's Hospital.

In October 1776, when undercover agent Enoch Crosby began his espionage activities, he decided to bring his intelligence urgently to Youngs, whom he knew only by reputation. He arrived at the Four Corners home late at night. Just prior to that visit, Crosby, posing as a Loyalist, had infiltrated a Tory group that was forming in the central part of the county and gathering arms to strike at Patriot forces.[112]

About midnight, Crosby found Four Corners and conveyed his intelligence to Youngs, who, upon hearing it, immediately took Crosby into White Plains. The two men covered the four or five miles by foot, arriving at their destination at 2:00 a.m., where, despite the lateness of the hour, they met with John Jay, the political leader of the Patriots in the county. Jay acted expeditiously, and the Tories were found, disarmed and arrested.[113]

Crosby had intended to enlist in the Continental army, but Jay, impressed by the quality of Crosby's information, urged him to serve his country by continuing his undercover work instead. He agreed, and many dangerous adventures followed. But Crosby was skilled at espionage and survived the war.

February 3, 1780: The Attack on the Youngs House—A Demoralizing Blow

The Youngs house became an active American militia post, and the British began to target it with strikes that became more and more destructive. The raid of February 1780 was the worst and was carefully planned. Detachments of British and Hessian regular troops, and Delancey's Royal Refugees (Loyalist Americans), cooperated in the operation and attacked in deep snow on February 3.[114] There were about 650 raiders in all. The American defenders, for the most part Massachusetts regiments, were greatly outnumbered, comprising only 250 men. Westchester Patriots were about to suffer one of the severest losses of the war.[115]

Setting out from Kingsbridge at 10:30 p.m. on an extremely cold night, the attackers were obliged to march twenty miles over snow-covered roads and fields, and they didn't arrive in the vicinity of their target until 9:30 a.m. A Patriot scout who saw them was able to speed to the house and give the military commander there, Colonel Thompson, a few minutes forewarning.

The American defenders were not all concentrated at the house, however. Many were stationed at outposts on the east–west crossroad, known today as Grasslands Road. These were the men who encountered the enemy first, and when they did, they found themselves dealing with a crack grenadier regiment. Nevertheless, they held them off until their commander, Captain Moses Roberts, fell.

The Hessians were on the left side of the attacking column and approached Youngs Corners from the area that serves now as the roadbed of the Sprain Brook Parkway.[116] The British regulars and their Loyalist auxiliaries were on the right and attacked the Patriot house from the area now occupied by Westchester Community College and the residential neighborhood adjacent to the college.

In short order, the defenders were overwhelmed. The house was burned, and Four Corners became known for several years thereafter as the site of "the Burnt House." Nineteen of its defenders were killed. Ninety-three were taken prisoner and marched to New York.

Youngs was among the captured men. It was the second time he had been seized by the British and marched off to detention in New York City.

Left: Plaque honoring American defenders of Youngs Corners, attacked on February 3, 1780. *Author's photo*.

Below: Battle of Youngs Corners monument, located on Grasslands Road, about two hundred yards west of Youngs (or Four) Corners. *Author's photo*.

Gravestone of Joseph Youngs
in the cemetery of Old Dutch
Church, Sleepy Hollow, New York.
Author's photo.

Like many other Patriot prisoners, he was confined in the "Old Sugar
House," a terribly overcrowded institution where captured American
soldiers tried to survive under the miserable conditions that prevailed.
Other prisoners of war were confined in the infamous prison ships of
New York Harbor, where conditions were even more abysmal.

Youngs managed to survive both his period of detention and the war.
He lived until March 1789, long enough to see New York State ratify the
new U.S. Constitution.

Chapter 5

NOW OR NEVER
OUR DELIVERANCE
MUST COME

By January 1, 1781, the day the Pennsylvania line mutinied, thirty-eight months had passed since the spectacular American victory at Saratoga. It was expected that the fortunes of the United States would improve after Saratoga, and it is true that the victory there led to the French alliance and to open military assistance from the French government.

Yet over the course of those thirty-eight months, the benefits of Saratoga seemed to fade steadily away. Perhaps most surprising, the advantages of the French alliance appeared less certain with each passing year. After the formation of the alliance in February 1778, each attempt of French naval forces to assist the Americans had ended in failure and disappointment.

THE UNCOOPERATIVE STATES

The problems faced by the Americans went well beyond those disappointments. The Continental army was destitute. It was an army in rags. Congress, insolvent, did not have the means to pay the Continental soldiers or to supply them with adequate food and clothing. Washington did not blame the penniless Congress for the sorry condition of the army. But he did blame the states, and especially those states that had functioning economies. Yes, they were all suffering from the war, but many states clearly had the wherewithal to support the American army.

In his correspondence, Washington did not hold back; state officials were risking dishonor and disgrace. Writing to the president of Congress the previous July, Washington let it be known that time was running out for the American cause. If the states did not do their duty on behalf of their own liberty, the cause would be defeated and the states would be remembered in ignominy: "The die is cast, and it remains with the states to fulfill their engagements, to preserve their credit, and support their independence or involve us in disgrace and defeat."[117]

He refused to let his letter end on a despondent note: "I shall proceed on the supposition that they will ultimately consult their own interest and Honor and not suffer us to fail for want of means which it is evidently in their power to afford."[118]

Perhaps they ultimately would, but in the new year there was little evidence of it. Why were the states not providing their quota of troops? Why were they not provisioning the army with the most basic necessities? Did they not value their liberty? Their independence? Neither had been secured, and neither *would* be secured without military success. Did the states not understand this? The political leaders in the states all too often responded feebly to Washington's appeals, providing only meager assistance to the army. In one case, there was no response at all. In May and June 1781, he wrote letter after letter to Governor John Hancock of Massachusetts Bay, asking for provisions and troops, but Hancock did not even reply. Finally, on July 8, Washington protested:

Head Quarters near Dobbs's ferry[119]
Sir: I have not been honored with an answer to my several letters of the 24th and 25th of May and of the 2d. 4th 15th and 25th of last Month, and am of course unable to form any certain estimate of what may be expected in consequence of my requisitions. This puts me in a rather awkward situation, as I cannot give His Excellency Count Rochambeau, who has formed a junction with me, that official assurance of support which I had promised upon the faith of the states.[120]

The Encampment on the Hudson and the Trapping of Cornwallis

John Hancock, 1765, John
Singleton Copley, American.
*Photograph © 2011 Museum of
Fine Arts, Boston.*

In his 1805 biography of George Washington, Supreme Court chief justice John Marshall described the "state of affairs at the beginning of the year 1781":

> *The deep gloom which had enveloped the prospects of America in the commencement of the year, which darkened for a time in the south, had also spread itself over the north. The total incompetency of the political system adopted by the United States to their own preservation, became every day more apparent. Each state seemed fearful of doing too much, and of taking upon itself a larger portion of the common burden than was borne by its neighbour.*[121]

Small wonder that historian Stanley Klos writes that by the end of 1780, more than three years after the victory at Saratoga, "the fortunes of the Americans, instead of improving, had grown worse to the point of desperation."[122]

The Mutiny of the Pennsylvania Line

Encamped near Morristown, New Jersey, the Pennsylvania men began their mutiny on the night of January 1 by seizing several cannon and defying their officers, wounding several and killing one captain.[123]

The men argued that because they had enlisted "for three years or the war," their term of service had expired when the three years were up, on December 31. While this argument was technically weak, since they were ignoring the three words "or the war," they did have many legitimate grievances, primary among them chronic arrears of pay and chronic insufficiency of clothing and food. They blamed the Congress for these privations and decided to march on Philadelphia and compel the Congress to meet their demands.

The mutiny of New Year's Day confronted Washington with many dilemmas. Encamped with the main army at New Windsor, near West Point, he could not himself act against the mutineers. For one thing, he lacked the food and transportation that would be needed to move his army.[124] Moreover, he could not abandon West Point, rendering it vulnerable to capture by the enemy. Most worrying, he had to ask whether the mutineers might defect to the British and whether the spirit of mutiny might spread to other units, even to the main army itself.

On January 5, he sent the following circular letter to the governors of New Hampshire, Massachusetts, Rhode Island and Connecticut:

> *The aggravated calamities and distresses that have resulted to the soldiers from the total want of pay for nearly twelve months, the want of clothing at a severe season, and not infrequently the want of provisions, are beyond description.*
>
> *I give it decidedly as my opinion that it is vain to think an army can be kept together much longer under such a variety of sufferings as ours has experienced, and that unless some immediate and Spirited measures are adopted to furnish at least three months' pay to the troops in money… and at the same time ways and means are devised to clothe and feed them better (more regularly I mean) than they have been, the worst that can befall us may be expected.*[125]

The news that came into Washington's headquarters from officers reporting on the mutinous troops contained at least one positive element: the mutineers were expressing contempt for the idea that they might go over to the enemy, insisting that they "spurned the idea of turning into *Arnolds*." They proved the point by arresting two agents who had arrived on the scene from Sir Henry Clinton and who were offering them appealing terms if they would defect.[126]

Congress, frightened by the mutiny, quickly formed a committee of three to consult with Pennsylvania authorities on how to deal with it. The committeemen and state officials decided to negotiate with the mutineers, who had marched as far as Princeton. The uprising, then, would be dealt with by civilian officials. Throughout the war, Washington held it as a fundamental principle that Congress's authority was supreme in the land, second only to that of the sovereign people. He was the servant of Congress and unquestionably would accept the results of their negotiations.

After several days, a settlement was reported, and when Washington learned the details, while he accepted the terms, he feared their potential consequences. The civilian officials had capitulated on the essential matter of enlistment. The stipulation "for the war" would be ignored. Moreover, in cases where enlistment papers were missing, and there were many such cases, the soldier who swore an oath that his enlistment term had expired would be discharged. Washington foresaw that the arrangement would have a "very pernicious influence on the whole Army."[127]

THE MUTINY OF THE NEW JERSEY LINE

His prediction soon proved correct. On January 21, the New Jersey line, encamped at Pompton Lakes, New Jersey, mutinied. This time, before civil authorities had a chance to intervene, Washington was determined to confront the mutineers, offer them no compromises and employ strict military discipline. Explaining his thinking to Congress, he wrote: "The spirit of mutiny will spread itself through the remainder of the Army, if not extinguished by some decisive measure...I shall...march a detachment to compel the mutineers to submission, and I beg leave strongly to recommend that no terms may be made with them."[128]

Washington chose General Robert Howe to carry out the mission, placing him in command of five to six hundred of the "most robust" men at West Point and telling him that "the object…is to compel the mutineers to unconditional submission…grant no terms while they are with arms in their hands in a state of resistance."[129]

Dr. James Thacher wrote, "It falls to my lot to accompany the detachment." Thanks to him, we have a clear narrative of the events that followed.[130] By the early morning of January 27, the detachment was eight miles from the camp of the mutineers. On that date:

> [We] marched…at one o'clock A.M…which brought us in view of the huts of the insurgent soldiers by dawn of day…General Howe next ordered his aid-de-camp to command the mutineers to appear on parade in front of their huts unarmed, within five minutes; observing them to hesitate, a second messenger was sent, and they instantly obeyed the command, and paraded in a line without arms, being in number between two and three hundred. Finding themselves closely encircled and unable to resist, they quietly submitted to the fate which awaited them. General Howe ordered that three of the ringleaders should be selected as victims for condign punishment. These unfortunate culprits were tried on the spot, Colonel Sprout being president of the court-martial, standing on the snow, and they were sentenced to be immediately shot. Twelve of the most guilty mutineers were next selected to be their executioners. This was a most painful task; being themselves guilty, they were greatly distressed with the duty imposed on them, and when ordered to load, some of them shed tears. The wretched victims, overwhelmed by the terrors of death, had neither time nor power to implore the mercy and forgiveness of their God, and such was their agonizing condition, that no heart could refrain from emotions of sympathy and compassion.[131]

Two of the ringleaders were then executed, and "the third being less criminal, by the recommendation of his officers, to his unspeakable joy, received a pardon."

> This tragical scene produced a dreadful shock, and a salutary effect on the minds of the guilty soldiers. Never were men more completely

humbled and penitent; tears of sorrow and of joy rushed from their eyes, and each one appeared to congratulate himself that his forfeited life had been spared...General Howe...then...addressed the whole line by platoons, endeavoring to impress their minds with a sense of the enormity of their crime, and the dreadful consequences that might have resulted. He then commanded them...to devote themselves to the faithful discharge of their duty as soldiers in future. It is most painful to reflect that circumstances should imperiously demand the infliction of capital punishment on soldiers who have more than a shadow of plea to extenuate their crime. The success of the Pennsylvania insurgents undoubtedly encouraged them to hope for exemption from punishment. But the very existence of an army depends on proper discipline and subordination...The spirit of revolt must be effectually repressed, or a total annihilation of the army is inevitable.[132]

AMBASSADOR LUZERNE CAUTIONS CONGRESS: THE STRUGGLE FOR INDEPENDENCE CANNOT BE SUSTAINED INDEFINITELY

The emergency was over, and the worst had been avoided: the immediate threat of the army's disintegration had been averted. Relieved, Washington and Congress could put the acute crisis behind them and focus once more on their chronic, unremitting troubles.

Time was not on the side of the Americans. The 1781 campaign would almost certainly be the last chance to win independence. A year before, in January 1780, Congress was cautioned by the French ambassador, the Chevalier de Luzerne, that the allied struggle for American independence could not be sustained indefinitely. He told the delegates that the French king wished "to impress upon the minds of Congress that the British cabinet have an almost insuperable reluctance to admit the idea of the independence of these United States and will use every possible endeavor to prevent it." By itself, this observation could hardly have been surprising, but it was accompanied by another: M. Luzerne stated that "should the enemy be in possession of any part of these United States at the close of the next campaign, it will be extremely difficult to bring

Great Britain to acknowledge their independence."[133] In other words, the next campaign would be decisive. If the British could claim control of any state, or portion of any state, following that campaign, it was very likely that those territories would remain British possessions and would not become independent.

UTI POSSIDETIS

I confess I should dread a negotiation for a general peace at this time, because I should expect propositions for short truces, uti possidetis *and other conditions.* [134]
—John Adams, writing in 1781

[It was] *the most insidious and dangerous plot that was ever laid to ensnare us and deprive us of our independence. I mean the projected Congress at Vienna and the mediation of the two Imperial Courts, the Emperor of Germany and the Empress of Russia. This great event is wholly unknown to the Public in America, but it will be one day explained.* [135]
—John Adams, writing in 1809 and recalling the mediation proposal of 1781

In May 1780, Ambassador Luzerne provided more detail. He explained to Congress that following the next campaign (this seemed to mean the campaign of 1781), a territorial division could be expected, and that the boundaries between the warring parties would be determined by Russian and Austrian mediators (and, as John Adams stated in 1809, perhaps German mediators as well) at a conference in Vienna, where the mediators would apply the principle of *uti possidetis*, which in Latin means "as you possess it."[136]

Implementing that principle, the mediators would draw the boundaries of the United States in accordance with current battle lines, and the United States would consist only of the territory that its military controlled at the moment of the armistice.[137]

In the early months of 1781, the American military could claim control of most of the territory east of the Alleghenies and north of

The Encampment on the Hudson and the Trapping of Cornwallis

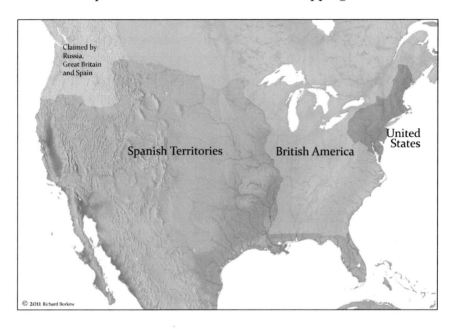

Possible boundaries of the United States under *uti possidetis* provisions, if determined on the basis of the military stalemate in the spring of 1781. Copyright 2011 by Richard Borkow.

Virginia, with the notable exceptions of New York City and Long Island. In the southern states, it would not have been clear where the fluid battle lines ought to be drawn, and the mediators at Vienna would be free to use their own criteria when they attempted to apply the criterion of *uti possidetis* to the south. British control of major cities in Georgia and the Carolinas, and the collapse of the government in Virginia after the raids of Arnold, Phillips and later Cornwallis, would probably be given great weight by the mediators. Although British control of the Carolina countryside was hotly contested by Patriot militia bands in 1781, ambiguities of that sort would probably not have mattered much to unsympathetic imperial courts.

Uti possidetis, as interpreted by the European powers, would most likely have meant a vulnerable, truncated United States, hemmed in near the coast, with Great Britain retaining the trans-Allegheny west, New York City, Long Island and the four southernmost states.[138]

An armistice under *uti possidetis* would not necessarily compel the British to recognize the independence of the diminished United States, and it would permit the French to leave the alliance. Great Britain would be positioned to renew hostilities against the American republic at any time of its choosing. As John Adams understood, a peace arrangement under those terms meant dismal prospects for the thirteen United States. Their independence was about to be bartered away in distant Vienna.

THE PLIGHT OF VIRGINIA

The possibility that the entire South might be lost as the result of a mediated settlement, including his home state of Virginia, greatly vexed the commander in chief.[139] If the terms at a Vienna conference would eventually depend on effective military control in each of the thirteen American states, then the news from south of the Potomac was not encouraging. Britain's southern strategy had achieved alarming successes in 1780, and the first news of 1781 did not promise much improvement. Arnold had arrived in Virginia with a sizable force on or about January 1, and local forces there proved powerless to resist him. He quickly dominated the James River Valley, ravaging the countryside, setting fire to storehouses, burning seagoing craft and destroying vast supplies of tobacco and flour. As the weeks passed, there was no relief. On the contrary, from January through March, when Arnold was joined by General Alexander Phillips, the prospects for Virginia only seemed to worsen.

Moreover, British domination in Virginia, the gateway to the three southernmost states, would threaten communication with General Nathanael Greene, whose diverse forces, composed of regular troops and various homegrown militias, were struggling in the Carolinas with the British and Hessian troops of the Earl of Eyre, Lord Cornwallis. British control of Virginia would also threaten Greene's supplies. If provisions could not get to him through Virginia, he would have to depend entirely on local sources to continue his resistance.

As the assault on Virginia continued into the spring and summer of 1781, Washington focused again and again on the state's ordeal and tried to conceive of ways to rescue it. Virginia officials wrote to him, pleading that he rush to his native state as its defender. He had to be circumspect

General Cornwallis, artist
unknown. *From* Diary of
the American Revolution
*(New York: Charles T. Evans,
1863) Frank Moore, ed.*

in his replies, but the fact was that he could not march south with the army. The army didn't have the means to undertake such a march. Nor could he come to Virginia himself without it. He needed to be with the Continental army and close to Rochambeau, to confer with him and to develop a war-winning strategy with him. It was unquestionably true that the French alliance, whatever the disappointments of the past, still offered America its best chance for victory.

To one Virginia correspondent, he wrote in June:

> *Nobody…can doubt my inclination to be immediately employed in the defense of that country where all my property and connections are; but there are powerful objections to my leaving the Army at this time, but neither time nor prudence will allow me to go into detail of them on paper; one only I will name, which is that no other person has the power to command the French troops.*

By June, Washington had reason to be especially attentive to prudence in his letter writing, for three months earlier, in mid-March, he had penned a highly indiscreet letter complaining about the French, and it had been intercepted by British agents. In the intercepted correspondence, Washington had groused to his cousin, Lund Washington, that the French had squandered an opportunity to assist Virginia. To Washington's great embarrassment, the letter was then published in New York in the Tory press at Sir Henry Clinton's direction, who hoped that its publication would promote a rift between the allies. Washington's incautious remarks were now known far and wide.

The First Battle of the Capes

The events that led to the indiscreet letter started to take shape in January 1781 as the result of an unexpected meteorological event. The English fleet, which had been cooping up the French warships at Newport, was suddenly disabled by a major storm and had to limp back to New York to be refitted. The waters of Newport Harbor had remained relatively calm, and the French vessels at anchorage there were undamaged. In the immediate aftermath of the storm, the French ships were free to leave the harbor unmolested.

From Washington's point of view, the storm had given the allies an unexpected opportunity to save Virginia and, at the same time, to capture the traitor Arnold. He envisioned the French fleet sailing rapidly from Newport to the Chesapeake Bay, an American column marching rapidly south, and the two converging at Portsmouth, where Arnold had his base. The traitor would be trapped between them, his army defeated and Virginia rescued. But quick action was essential. As soon as the British vessels had been reconstituted in New York Harbor, the French naval advantage would be lost.

To execute this plan, Washington rushed 1,200 men on February 19 under Lafayette's command from the Hudson Highlands to Virginia and simultaneously wrote to Rochambeau, suggesting to him and to his naval chief, the Chevalier Destouches,[140] that the entire Newport fleet (eight ships of the line) be dispatched to the Chesapeake Bay without delay to cooperate with Lafayette.

The entire French fleet did not depart from Newport until March 8. But weeks earlier, before Washington's suggestions had arrived at Newport, the French had acted independently by sending a small expedition—three vessels—to the Chesapeake. The little squadron was sent with a modest objective. Not capable of defeating Arnold, the flotilla intended merely to cause some disruption to his shipping. The dispatch of the three vessels delayed implementation of Washington's much more ambitious proposal, for the French were not able to send out their entire fleet until the small expedition had returned to Newport.

But by March 8, when all eight French ships of the line left Newport, the shipwrights at New York Harbor had completed their repairs. The British ships were now refitted and ready for action. Their commanders in New York surmised that the departing French vessels were headed for the Chesapeake, and the British warships set sail after them.[141] As Washington saw it, the French had dawdled the time away and missed a precious window of opportunity.

The two fleets headed south at roughly the same time and met in mid-March at the mouth of the Chesapeake Bay, where they fought what is now known as the first Battle of the Capes. In the engagement, the two sides sustained about equal damage, and the action ended inconclusively. However, the British managed to occupy Chesapeake Bay, and Destouches did not have the means to drive them out. Since the French ships were not able to enter the bay and approach Portsmouth, they returned to Newport. Lafayette had been able to reach Virginia fairly quickly with his 1,200 men. But his force, even when supplemented with Virginia militia, was much weaker than Arnold's, and there was little the marquis could do without the help of the French fleet.

Yet the planning of this naval and land operation early in 1781 was not entirely a wasted effort, for it brought Lafayette into Virginia, where he remained with his army. His continuing presence there enabled him to keep track of British military activities, and he periodically sent intelligence back to Washington. By the time of the Lower Westchester Encampment in the summer of 1781, Lafayette's reports about British army movements in Virginia, rushed by couriers to the Hudson, were highly beneficial to the allied commanders as they weighed their options and planned the line of attack that would prove to be the most decisive of the war.

THE DENOUEMENT OF THE "INDISCREET LETTER" IMBROGLIO AND AN UPDATE SENT TO COLONEL JOHN LAURENS IN PARIS

Washington wrote several indiscreet letters to associates lamenting the outcome of the first Battle of the Capes and criticizing the performance of the French. Only one of them, the letter to his cousin, Lund, was intercepted and published by the British, and one was more than enough.[142] Upon reading the letter in the New York press, Rochambeau sent a letter of protest (albeit courteously phrased) to Washington and gave the American an out: had not the letter been forged? Washington declined to deny authorship. No, the letter had not been a forgery, he replied to Rochambeau, but perhaps it had been "written in haste and inaccurately expressed." He told the French commander that he felt "extreme pain" that the letter had been intercepted and made public. It was not a full-fledged apology, and James Thomas Flexner, Washington's biographer, suggests the reason why: the American general, he says, was still irritated that an exceptional opportunity had been lost.[143]

Writing in early April to Colonel John Laurens, the twenty-six-year-old South Carolinian who had been sent to Paris as Congress's emissary to plead for a loan from the French government, Washington brought the colonel up to date on recent events in America, including the failed Destouches expedition. He then turned to the vital importance of Laurens's mission in Paris and described an America under great duress:

> *Be assured my dear Laurens, that day does not follow night more certainly, than it brings with it some additional proof of the impracticability of carrying on the War without the aids you were directed to solicit...If France delays a timely and powerful aid in the critical posture of our affairs, it will avail us nothing should she attempt it hereafter...our Troops are approaching fast to nakedness...we have nothing to cloath them with... our Hospitals are without medicines, and our Sick without Nutriment... all our public works are at a stand, and the Artificers disbanding...*
>
> *But why need I run into the detail, when it may be declared in a word, that we are at the end of our tether, and that now or never our deliverance must come.*[144]

CONFLICT WITHIN THE BRITISH HIGH COMMAND

Relations between Washington and Rochambeau may have been strained by the fallout from the first Battle of the Capes, but this never seriously threatened to disrupt the alliance. They were both self-assured men, and it was difficult to wound them. The British commanders were not so self-assured and suffered from more fragile egos. This led them to express increasingly bitter feelings toward one another over the course of 1781 and, fortunately for the American cause, contributed to strategic missteps, some of which proved significant to the outcome of the war.

Because of the dramatic British victories at Savannah in 1779 and Charleston and Camden in 1780, George Germain, the American minister in London, was convinced that the southern strategy had already proven itself and would inevitably lead to recovery of all the southern provinces. It is not clear how fully apprised he was of subsequent British defeats and difficulties in controlling the southern states. While the Crown maintained its hold on the major southern seaports in 1781, the countryside was becoming more and more insecure. When the southern strategy started to collapse, stark and bitter differences emerged between Germain, Clinton and Cornwallis.

By the latter months of 1780, the guerrilla forces of Marion (the Swamp Fox), Sumter and Pickens were making the countryside in North and South Carolina extremely dangerous for the British, cutting off communication between posts, staging raids on foraging parties and overcoming contingents of Loyalist militia. The Americans, moreover, started to win major battles, most notably at Kings Mountain in western North Carolina in October 1780 and at Cowpens, near present-day Spartanburg, South Carolina, in January 1781.

In the contest between the British commander in the South, Lord Cornwallis, and the American commander, Nathanael Greene, the latter was considerably more successful. Greene understood that he could weaken Cornwallis simply by avoiding major defeats himself and by drawing the British army deep into the interior, far from its sources of supplies at the coastal cities. In March 1781, Cornwallis sustained huge losses at the Battle of Guilford Courthouse (despite a technical victory there). He lost more than a quarter of his men in the battle and was forced to march his battered army two hundred miles to the coast to recover.

In London, parliamentarian Charles James Fox, an opponent of the American war, said: "Another such victory would ruin the British army!"[145] While Cornwallis might not admit the validity of Fox's comment, implicitly he seemed to agree with it. Two months after Guilford Courthouse, he fled the scene, abandoning the Carolinas, even though the British position in those states had clearly become quite shaky.

Cornwallis decided that the answer lay in Virginia, the most prosperous of the southern states. Rebel resistance in the states farther south was being aided by supplies from Virginia. Cornwallis argued that the resistance was dependent on that aid and that the rebellion in the Carolinas and Georgia could not sustain itself if support from Virginia were cut off. The earl therefore resolved to leave the Carolinas and deal with Virginia directly. He would march his army into that state, confront the rebels there, interrupt the state's economy and undermine the southern rebellion at its source. It was a debatable proposition, but it served as a convenient pretext to justify his exit from the chaotic Carolinas.

GERMAIN: THE REBEL FORCE IS NOW SO VERY CONTEMPTIBLE

Lord Germain, who had overall responsibility for the war strategy, failed to acknowledge these troublesome developments in the Carolinas and Georgia. In December 1780, writing about the rebel resistance "in all parts"—i.e., in North and South alike—he offered this assessment: "So very contemptible is the rebel force now in all parts, and so vast is our superiority, that no resistance on their part is to be apprehended that can materially obstruct the progress of the King's arms in the speedy suppression of the rebellion."[146]

And a few months later, in the spring of 1781, Germain wrote to Cornwallis:

> *I make no doubt your Lordship will, by this time, have had the honor to recover the province of North Carolina to his Majesty; and I am even*

sanguine enough to hope, from your Lordship's distinguished abilities and zeal for the Kings service, that the recovery of part of Virginia will crown your success before the season becomes too intemperate for land operations.[147]

Germain's remarks failed to take account of some important facts. For example, in the spring of 1781, Lieutenant Colonel Balfour, commander of the British garrison in Charleston , wrote the following to Clinton:

I must inform Your Excellency that the general state of the country is most distressing and that the enemy's parties are everywhere. The communication by land with Savannah no longer exists. Colonel Brown is invested [besieged] at Augusta, and Colonel Cruger in the most critical situation at Ninety Six. Indeed, I should betray the duty I owe Your Excellency did I not represent the defection of this province as so universal that I know of no mode short of depopulation to retain it.

CLINTON V. GERMAIN

Almost simultaneously Henry Clinton, bemoaning the absence of effective Loyalist support in the rebelling provinces, sent the following dose of reality to Germain: "Experience ought to convince us that there is no possibility of restoring order in any rebellious provinces on this continent without the hearty assistance of numerous friends. These, my Lord, I think are not to be found in Virginia nor dare I say under present circumstances that they are to be found anywhere else."[148]

While Clinton doubted the utility of an offensive approach by 1781, he had reason for some confidence that a defensive strategy would redound to the benefit of Great Britain. Referring to the contents of still another intercepted letter, Sir Henry wrote:

The most interesting piece of intelligence that this capture procured us was an intimation from the court of France that this was the last campaign in which the Americans were to expect assistance of either troops or ships from that nation…strongly pointing out to us the policy of avoiding all risks as much as possible, because it was now manifest that if we could only persevere in escaping affront, Time alone would soon bring about every success we could wish.[149]

Clinton was making a cogent point. Time was on the side of Great Britain, if only it could forbear, hold fast to its present possessions and not risk them through recklessly aggressive actions. It was an intelligent appraisal of the new situation, completely unacceptable to Germain and to Cornwallis.

Clinton also was reluctant to move British armies far from the coast. Campaigns deep in the interior of America would separate British armies from naval protection and deprive them of ready access to the abundant supplies that the British fleet could provide. From Clinton's point of view, it was safest for Britain to set up its fortifications on the coast and foolish for any British army to throw away the advantages of naval support. Lord Cornwallis ignored that principle and discarded those advantages when he chased after General Nathanael Greene in the interior of North Carolina in late 1780 and early 1781. Cornwallis's army and the British war effort in America suffered greatly because of that imprudent decision.

CORNWALLIS V. CLINTON

Without authorization from Clinton, Cornwallis put his Virginia plan into execution and marched his troops into Virginia in May 1781. When Clinton learned of the move into Virginia, he was appalled. Cornwallis had taken a major action without his knowledge, let alone his concurrence. Did Cornwallis not recognize that Clinton was commander in chief?

In a letter to Cornwallis on May 29, 1781, Clinton complained: "In the disordered state of Carolina and Georgia, I shall dread what shall be the consequence of your Lordship's move…but what is done cannot now be altered." And on June 8, still smarting from Cornwallis's unauthorized move into Virginia, Clinton wrote this reprimand: "I am persuaded that I need not say to your Lordship how necessary it is that I should be informed without delay of every change in position in your Lordship's army."

Cornwallis launched a series of effective raids against Patriot strong points in Virginia. On one of them, Banastre Tarleton's dragoons nearly captured Virginia governor Thomas Jefferson at his home in Monticello. Had Cornwallis been permitted to continue in this mode, he might have given the floundering southern strategy new life. But Clinton, who was becoming very concerned about the impending junction of Washington and Rochambeau in lower Westchester, made demands on Cornwallis that could only serve to wreck his Virginia strategy.

DOBBS FERRY AND THE 1781 ENCAMPMENT

In early May, Washington received several dispatches from Rochambeau and other French commanders at Newport that brought significant news: the French frigate *Concord* had just arrived in Boston, and important military personages had disembarked, most notably Rochambeau's son,[150] who had been conferring at Versailles, and Admiral Comte de Barras, who had come to take charge of the Newport fleet, replacing the Chevalier Destouches. The commander's son had important information, including the prospect of significant involvement in the near future by the French navy, a large component of which had already left France. The communications from Newport emphasized that the new information must be shared with the American commander in chief, and Rochambeau urged another meeting at the earliest possible date.

General Chastellux, one of the commanders at Newport, wrote to Washington that help would soon be coming from France and that Rochambeau would suggest that the French army march to the Hudson "for joint operations."[151]

Rochambeau had known for almost a year that Washington had established a communication post on the Hudson at Dobbs Ferry. Its purpose, Washington said, was to get the armies close to New York in case the city became their "eventual object" in a joint attack. The American commander had first written to him about it on August 5, 1780: "The Army is recrossing the river and will proceed to Dobbs ferry, about 10 miles from Kingsbridge where we intend to establish a communication that will save us considerable land transportation, in case New York is our eventual object."

A few days later, Washington had sent a similar communication to General William Heath, who was in Rhode Island with Rochambeau, serving as the French general's official military host in America: "We are now going, agreeably to my original design, to establish as soon as possible a communication for the present across the river at Dobbs' Ferry, in order to aid our land transportation and facilitate our supplies of bread."[152]

And on August 11, 1780, Washington had ordered General Benedict Arnold, who was then the new commander at West Point, to supply sixty "Artificers"[153] for the construction of the Dobbs Ferry works: "We shall have occasion to throw up some small works at Dobbs' Ferry, to secure the intended communication at that place; and in order that we may be enabled to finish them in the most expeditious manner, you will be pleased to order sixty of Colonel Baldwin's Artificers to come immediately down here."[154]

Those orders had been given to Arnold just nine months before. Since then, so much had happened, and almost all the news, month after month, had been dismaying. But now in May 1781, there were finally some very good tidings! Apparently, the French navy was now prepared to contribute in a major way to the 1781 campaign; and Rochambeau would be able to join forces with him on the Hudson close to New York.

Washington suggested that they confer on May 21 at Wethersfield, Connecticut.[155] It would be the third meeting of the allied commanders and would lay the groundwork for the Lower Westchester Encampment.

Chapter 6

TO NEW YORK OR TO VIRGINIA?

Prior to their conference at Wethersfield (May 21–22, 1781),[156] Generals Washington and Rochambeau had essentially agreed that the Continental and French armies would soon meet on the Hudson. But they hadn't agreed on what would happen after that. Where would they concentrate their combined forces for joint operations? The choice came down to New York or Virginia. Would Sir Henry Clinton's stronghold on Manhattan or the British-Hessian forces in Virginia be the most suitable objective for the allied armies? That was the main item for discussion at Wethersfield.

Rochambeau argued for a march of the allied armies to Virginia. Since the French would start in Rhode Island, they would have to march more than six hundred miles in order to reach Virginia. The distance for the Americans would be more than four hundred miles. The comte proposed to join Washington at the Hudson River and then proceed south, alongside the Americans, from the Hudson to Virginia's Chesapeake region.

Washington did not agree. He wanted the two armies to combine forces on the Hudson for an attack on British New York. If an American and French attack on New York succeeded, it would smash British power at its North American hub and be the most decisive victory of the war. As to Virginia, he questioned the practicality of so long a march. The foremost problem was lack of resources, for a march to the South would be prohibitively expensive. The Continental army simply didn't have the funds to pay the costs of transportation. Even assuming, hypothetically, that the money could be found, Washington questioned whether his troops, many of them New Englanders, would accept a march of more than four hundred miles in the summer heat to a southern climate that many soldiers from those four northern states considered malarial and lethal. To put it bluntly, Washington was afraid that large numbers would desert along the way.[157]

Summing up, the commander in chief wrote the following to Rochambeau: "The great waste of men which we have found from experience in the long marches in the southern states...the difficulty of transport by land—and others too well known to the Count de Rochambeau to need repeating, show that an operation against New York should be preferred in the present circumstances."[158]

A Long-standing Controversy

Ever since the Wethersfield conference, the debate that took place there between the commanders has been a source of historical controversy. Because the Virginia option eventually led to the siege of Yorktown, the surrender of General Cornwallis and victory in the war, some contend that Rochambeau, and not Washington, ought to get the credit for backing the war-winning strategy at Wethersfield.

However, it is difficult to imagine that either Washington or Rochambeau, in late May 1781, anticipated the steps that would eventually win the war. Yes, Cornwallis was in Virginia at the time of the Wethersfield meeting. He had just marched there from North Carolina. His first stop, on May 20, was at Petersburg. There he assumed command of Arnold's 3,000-man army and merged his 1,500 troops with it.[159] But at Wethersfield, the allied commanders could not have been aware of any of those important facts.

What Did They Know, and When Did They Know It?

News took a long time to travel in 1781, and the allied generals learned about Cornwallis's presence in Virginia only after they were back at their respective headquarters in New Windsor and Newport, following the

Wethersfield conference. Lafayette dispatched a flurry of communications to Washington about Cornwallis's arrival, reporting, in a May 17 letter, on the earl's impending appearance at Petersburg and sending updates on May 18 and May 24. Washington received the letters from Lafayette by June 3, about a week after he had returned from Wethersfield to his headquarters in New Windsor, on the Hudson.[160]

For several weeks thereafter, reports from Virginia placed Cornwallis in the interior of the state, far from the Chesapeake Bay. Once Washington and Rochambeau learned that Cornwallis was in the interior of Virginia, they had good reason to expect that he would stay there, since he was largely successful in his marauding operations in the interior.

The timing of Cornwallis's arrival in Virginia and the dates of Lafayette's letters have obvious implications for the historical controversy surrounding Wethersfield. One of the historians to elaborate on this theme is James Thomas Flexner, who relates that Rochambeau's memoirs, written several years later, described Washington as "myopic" at Wethersfield and oblivious to the possibility that Cornwallis could be trapped on the Virginia coast of the Chesapeake Bay. Flexner asserts that the French commander's recollection was faulty on that point and that at Wethersfield Rochambeau was no more aware than Washington that Cornwallis might eventually station himself at Yorktown—or anywhere else on the Chesapeake—and become trappable there.[161]

ROCHAMBEAU'S GOALS

In short, Cornwallis's army was not the target Rochambeau had in mind at Wethersfield when he advocated an allied march to Virginia. Nor was Yorktown the place. The French general intended that the allies seize Portsmouth, a British post at the mouth of the James River, manned by about 1,500 troops.[162] Since the British armies that were rampaging through the interior of Virginia relied on the shipping that entered Portsmouth, the loss of that port would do substantial harm to the Crown's forces in Virginia and to its strategy for that state.

Rochambeau felt that at New York the advantages were overwhelmingly on the British side. The city was strongly fortified, and a strike against Sir

Henry's Manhattan garrison had little chance of success, even if the fleet of French Admiral de Grasse, which had recently left France for the West Indies, were to participate in the attack. Rochambeau, logically enough, wanted to take action where the allies possessed strong advantages, and Portsmouth was such a place, especially if de Grasse's ships were on hand to lend assistance.

New York, Not Portsmouth, Would Be a Knockout Blow

For Washington, the choice of Virginia over New York presented a major problem in addition to the difficulties associated with a long march: while the capture of Portsmouth would undermine the enemy's position in Virginia, it would not deal the British the knockout blow that was needed now. This, after all, would be America's last chance. Rochambeau's army (and, the American commander hoped, de Grasse's fleet as well) gave Washington a one time only opportunity. With the aid of the French army and fleet, he had a chance to deliver the British such a shattering blow that his country's dismemberment at Vienna might be prevented. *The war might even be won.* For no greater triumph could be imagined than the defeat of the British at New York.

Washington: A New York Strategy Will Relieve the Ordeal of Virginia

Washington added that a concentration of American and French forces close to New York, if it accomplished nothing else, would nevertheless bring real relief, indirectly, to Virginia. The mere threat to attack New York, he predicted, would force Sir Henry Clinton to strengthen his defenses on Manhattan by withdrawing troops from the South and thereby "enfeeble [British] Southern operations."

Washington's prediction that Clinton would seek to withdraw troops from Virginia proved accurate. Yet, as it turned out, those troops were never actually withdrawn. The impact of Washington's New York strategy on British operations in Virginia would benefit the American cause even more than he imagined.

The Information that Was Withheld

At Wethersfield, both generals knew that Admiral de Grasse had recently arrived in the West Indies with a powerful fleet. But Rochambeau knew, in addition, something that he did not tell Washington: that de Grasse also had orders to bring his naval force from the West Indies to North American waters in the summer in order to assist the allied armies. In light of Washington's indiscreet letter just two months before, the count was apparently reluctant to mention that detail to the American. The risk that such important news would fall into the hands of the British, perhaps through another intercepted letter, seemed too great.[163] Washington of course *hoped* that a French fleet would arrive on the coast of the United States, but at Wethersfield he was able to speak about that possibility only in the hypothetical. Rochambeau knew that it would probably become a reality.

The Wethersfield Conference Concludes: New York Will Be the Primary Target, but Virginia Remains a Contingency If New York Fails

Washington stated that he was not opposed in all circumstances to an allied movement into Virginia. He recognized that everything would depend on future events, including the decisions made by the French naval commanders, Admiral de Grasse and Admiral de Barras (still in Newport). "Whatever efforts are made by the land armies," he said some weeks later, "the navy must have the casting vote in the present contest."[164] The admirals were independent of the generals and were free to make their own decisions.

If de Grasse were to bring his fleet to the coast of the United States during the 1781 campaign, Washington hoped he would sail first to Sandy Hook outside New York Harbor. If de Grasse's ships were unable to pass the bar at Sandy Hook, or if an attack against New York did not prove feasible for any other reason, the allies could then turn to the Virginia option. It would be desirable for de Grasse to come to New York first even if the allies ultimately were to choose the Virginia option. For in that circumstance, the allied armies could be transported quickly south on the admiral's ships, and the difficulties of transport by land that concerned Washington so greatly would no longer be an issue.

Rochambeau, his reservations about a New York strategy having been voiced, stated that he accepted the American commander's plan. He would join Washington in lower Westchester County by the Hudson River and, from there, probe for weaknesses in Sir Henry's Clinton's defenses on Manhattan.

In a diary entry at the conclusion of the Wethersfield conference, Washington summarized its results:

> [May] 22d. [1781] *Fixed with Count de Rochambeau upon plan of Campaign…that the French land force (except 200 men) should March… to the North River, and there, in conjunction with the American, to commence an operation against New York…or to extend our views to the southward as circumstances and a Naval superiority might render more necessary.*[165]

SIX MILLION LIVRES!

On May 26, one day after he returned from Wethersfield, Washington received a communication at his New Windsor headquarters from John Laurens in Paris. The young emissary's letter brought very heartening news: a donation of six million livres had recently been promised by the French government to support the American war effort in 1781.

That was not all. Laurens told Washington what Rochambeau had not, that Admiral de Grasse had orders to bring at least a portion of his fleet to the coast of the United States. The admiral was departing France, Laurens indicated, just as he was writing the letter and would bring a powerful armada to the West Indies. There de Grasse would have a double assignment: he had been instructed by the king to protect French and Spanish island possessions from the British, and he was also commanded to bring his ships to North America at some point during the summer and sweep British warships from the coast in cooperation with the plans of Washington and Rochambeau.

Most likely, Laurens wrote, the ships would appear off the shores of the United States in July.[166] They would consist of twelve sail of the line (so

Laurens had been told), detached for service on behalf of the American states, out of de Grasse's total of twenty.[167]

The six million livres had been promised by Charles Vergennes to Benjamin Franklin and was a tribute to the masterful diplomacy of the Pennsylvanian. It was also a sign of the determination of the French government to make an all-out effort to support the campaign of 1781.

"These People Are at the Very End of Their Resources"

Two weeks after he returned from Wethersfield to Newport, on June 11, Rochambeau sent a letter to Admiral de Grasse, the man whose decisions, probably more than those of any other key player, would determine success or failure in the 1781 campaign. The general suggested to the admiral that he would do well to bring his fleet to Virginia: "M. de Lafayette has not 1,000 regulars with the militia to defend Virginia... this is the state of affairs and the great crisis at which America finds itself...The southwesterly winds and the distressed state of Virginia will probably lead you to prefer Chesapeake Bay, and it is there that we think you can render the greatest services."[168]

Rochambeau also requested that de Grasse bring an additional 5,000 French troops to North America, explaining that: "These people are at the very end of their resources. Washington will not have at his disposal half of the number of troops he counted upon having. While he is secretive on this subject, I believe that at present he has not more than 6,000 men all told."[169]

Moody's Auspicious Interception

Shortly after Wethersfield, another letter of Washington's—this one to Lafayette—was intercepted by the British. The letter was sent on May 31 and was in Clinton's hands by the first week of June. In it Washington summarized the discussions at Wethersfield, writing that the allied armies planned to attack Manhattan, which, he said, would be their primary objective because *an attempt upon New York with its present garrison, which by estimation is reduced to 4,300 regular troops, and about 3,000 irregulars, was deemed preferable to a Southern Operation, as we had not command of the water. The reasons which induced this determination were the dangers to be apprehended from the approaching heats; the inevitable dissipation from the loss of men by a long march; and the difficulty of transportation—but above all it was thought we had a tolerable prospect of expelling the Enemy, or obliging them to withdraw part of their force from the southward, which would give most effective relief to those States.*[170]

This extremely informative communication was part of a packet of letters that was intercepted on June 3.[171] Fortunately, Washington's captured letter said nothing about the contingency plans regarding Virginia or about the possible arrival of de Grasse's fleet. That these omissions were deliberate for reasons of security is strongly intimated in his concluding words to Lafayette: "As you have no Cypher by which I can write you in safety, and my letters have been frequently intercepted of late, I refrain myself from mentioning many Matters that I wish to communicate to you."[172]

In his *Military Journal*, Dr. James Thacher named the captor of the packet and described his "artful and enterprising" methods:

It has several times happened that an artful and enterprising fellow, by the name of Moody,[173] *employed by the British in New York, has succeeded in taking our mail from the post rider on the road...After the interview of General Washington and Count Rochambeau, the British were particularly desirous of obtaining intelligence relative to the result. Accordingly, Moody was again despatched to effect the object. Being perfectly well acquainted with the roads and passes, he waylaid the mail for some days in the Jerseys, till at length it was his good fortune to possess himself of that very mail which contained General Washington's dispatches.*[174]

"THE MOST PERFECT KNOWLEDGE OF THE DESIGNS OF THE ENEMY"

Sir Henry could not refrain from boasting about the interception, and news of the letter's capture soon spread widely. Before long, an alarmed Congress "voted to change the route and to call on Washington to provide a mounted guard [for his couriers], something he could not [afford]."[175] Clinton was so pleased with Moody's achievement that he gave him a reward of two hundred guineas.

It was Moody's good fortune that he had gained possession of the mail, and it was also America's. Washington's letter, lengthy, logical and detailed, convinced Sir Henry that he now understood American and French strategy for 1781. The word in New York was that Moody had made one of the most important intelligence coups of the war. In Clinton's headquarters, Lieutenant Frederick McKenzie of the Royal Welsh fusiliers wrote in his diary: "The capture of this Mail is extremely consequential, and gives the Commander in Chief the most perfect knowledge of the designs of the Enemy."[176]

"I AM THREATENED WITH A SIEGE IN THIS POST"

In a June 11 letter to Cornwallis, Clinton told about the captured mail pouch, the alarming information contained therein and the dangers now faced by his New York bastion. He greatly exaggerated the size of the allied American and French troop strength that would be assembled against him in Westchester County, asserting that it would amount to at least 20,000 men (it would actually be 9,500) and insisting that Cornwallis weaken his forces in Virginia by sending a large reinforcement to New York.

After all, Cornwallis was in no real danger. Only paltry forces opposed him in Virginia: Lafayette's one thousand men, plus Anthony Wayne's army, most of whom, Clinton had been told, were ready to mutiny again, and the Virginia militia, who were "a small body of ill armed peasantry." As for Washington and Rochambeau, the letter that Moody captured revealed that "they have for the present no intention of sending reinforcements [to Virginia]."

Cornwallis would have to drop his present activities, leave the interior of Virginia and get his army to the coast where he should focus instead on establishing a safe harbor on the Chesapeake. Most important, Clinton instructed Cornwallis to detach a huge portion of his force, two thousand men, and place them on transports in the Chesapeake Bay bound for New York in order to contribute to the defense of the threatened city. Such a sizable dismantling of the British army in Virginia would completely undercut Cornwallis's ability to carry out his Virginia strategy.

Clinton was specific about the units that he needed in New York and about the best coastal cities to consider for a defensive post:

> *By the intercepted letters inclosed to your lordship in my last despatch, you will observe that I am threatened with a siege in this post...Thus circumstanced, I am persuaded your lordship will be of opinion, that the sooner I concentrate my force the better.*
>
> *Therefore, I beg leave to recommend it to you...to take a defensive station, in any healthy situation you choose, (be it at Williamsburg or York Town);[177] and...the following corps may be sent to me in succession, as you can spare them:*
>
> *Two battalions of light infantry; forty-third regiment; seventy-sixth or eightieth regiments; two battalions of Anspach; Queen's rangers, cavalry and infantry; remains of the detachment of the seventeenth light dragoons; and such proportion of artillery as can be spared, particularly men.*

Clinton ordered Cornwallis to be prepared to come to the aid of New York in a second way as well, by holding his army in readiness for an attack on Philadelphia. Such an attack would divert Washington and Rochambeau and reduce the danger to Manhattan.

"IT HAS BEEN SUBMITTED TO THE KING"

The very same day that Cornwallis received these demands to reinforce New York, Clinton himself received correspondence from George Germain that expressed London's strong approval for Cornwallis's attempts to subdue Virginia and upbraided Clinton for opposing it. Germain sternly reprimanded Clinton:

It was a great mortification to me to find that it appeared to be your intention that only a part of [British] troops should remain in the Chesapeake…Your ideas, therefore, of the importance of recovering that province [Virginia] appearing to be so different from mine, I thought it proper to ask the advice of his Majesty's other servants upon the subject, and their opinions concurring entirely with mine, it has been submitted to the King. And I am commanded by his Majesty to acquaint you that the recovery of the southern provinces and the prosecution of the war by pushing our conquests from south to north is to be considered the chief and principal object for the employment of all the forces under your command which can be spared from…defense.[178]

"Forever Liable to Become a Prey to a Foreign Enemy"

Upon receiving this rebuke, Clinton countermanded his earlier orders to Cornwallis. The two-thousand-man detachment that, by the time the countermand was received, had already been put on transports in Chesapeake Bay would eventually be disembarked and incorporated once more into Cornwallis's army. The commander in chief also dropped the idea of a diversionary strike against Philadelphia. But Clinton had succeeded in putting a stop to Cornwallis's Virginia aggressive strategy and was compelling him to adopt, instead, a defensive posture by setting up a naval base at Yorktown to protect British shipping in Chesapeake Bay.

Cornwallis argued passionately against the idea and on June 30 wrote to Clinton: "Upon viewing York [Yorktown] I was clearly of the opinion that it far exceeds our power, consistent with your plans, to make safe defensive posts there and at Gloucester, both of which would be necessary for the protection of shipping."[179]

Cornwallis reiterated his concerns in a July 8 letter to Clinton and revealed again how he much he disliked being confined to a defensive post on the coast:

I must again take the liberty of calling to your Excellency's serious attention the question of the validity of a defensive post in this country, which cannot have the smallest influence on the war in Carolina, and which only

gives us some acres of an unhealthy swamp, and is forever liable to become
a prey to a foreign enemy with a temporary superiority at sea.[180]

It must be said that Cornwallis was prescient about the liabilities associated with Yorktown. But Clinton was insistent, and Clinton was the commander in chief. Cornwallis had no choice but to comply, and on July 27, he wrote the following to Clinton: "I shall in obedience to the spirit of your Excellency's orders, take measures with as much despatch as possible to seize and fortify York [Yorktown] and Gloucester."

But Cornwallis took some revenge at the same time. He didn't know why Clinton had rescinded the orders for reinforcements. Fearing that the unpredictable commander in chief might renew those orders, Cornwallis tried to forestall that possibility by informing Clinton that Yorktown and Gloucester "command no country [and] a superiority in the field will not only be necessary to enable us to draw forage and other supplies from the country, but likewise to carry on our works without interruption."

"A superiority in the field" will be necessary! In other words, Clinton could forget about getting reinforcements from Virginia if he insisted on the fortification of such an unsuitable place as Yorktown.

So this bitter exchange between Clinton and Cornwallis set the stage. Yorktown would be fortified by Cornwallis against his will and against his better judgment. He would cease his aggressive actions in Virginia and could no longer hope to influence the "war in Carolina." Instead, his entire army of 7,500 British and Hessian troops would be put on defensive mode and in a location nearly impossible to defend if a foreign enemy should gain "a temporary superiority at sea."

From Lafayette's faithful and frequent correspondence, Washington and Rochambeau were kept apprised of Cornwallis's changing positions. But it was not until July, when the Continental and French armies were already bivouacked side by side in lower Westchester, that the allied commanders learned that Cornwallis had made his way east to the Chesapeake coast. From that time on, each successive letter from the marquis made it seem more and more likely that the British general was on the coast to stay. First he was at Williamsburg; then he moved to Jamestown, next to Portsmouth and finally to Yorktown.[181] If a French fleet were to gain control of Chesapeake Bay, these were all potentially trappable locations.

Chapter 7
THE ENCAMPMENT BY THE HUDSON

THE FRENCH MARCH TO THE NEW YORK BORDER

On June 10, with the departure of the First Brigade, the French expeditionary force began to leave Newport for Westchester County.[182] The brigade was conveyed by sail thirty miles north to Providence, which would be the actual starting point for the overland march. The Second Brigade followed on June 12.[183]

From Providence, Rochambeau's army started westward on June 18, with one regiment departing from the city each day. Since there were four regiments in all, the entire French force was on the move by June 21. Although the roads were terrible almost everywhere, they crossed the central parts of Rhode Island and Connecticut with impressive speed, on some days traveling by forced marches. The advance regiments reached East Hartford by June 23. The Legion of Lauzun marched separately, following a more southerly route through Connecticut, in order to cover the left flank of the main army.[184]

As they passed through one Yankee village after another—Plainfield, Windham, Bolton, Farmington—they made a dazzling display. The collars and coats of each regiment showed distinctive and brilliant colors, citron yellow, rose, crimson, green and sky blue, and the farmers and townsfolk came out to enjoy the spectacle.[185] For the most part, the

New Englanders were friendly and welcoming, and perhaps that is not surprising. These soldiers, after all, had come to rescue their country. Moreover, they were orderly and polite and paid for everything in hard money. But the friendliness of the population did represent a sea change in American attitudes toward the French, who, not too many years before, had been the arch enemies of the people of the thirteen British colonies, nowhere more so than in Puritan New England.

The French expeditionary force did not experience friendliness everywhere, however. After Farmington, the count's troops moved into southwestern Connecticut and approached the border of Westchester. The population in the border region must have been quite off-putting, because Baron von Closen wrote that that it was "full of Tories." And that was not the only problem. "The troops," von Closen went on, "suffered much hardship there, since they camped in a very stony field infested with snakes and adders. One soldier was bitten on the right arm and disabled by it."[186]

THE ASSAULT ON KINGSBRIDGE

In Newtown, Connecticut, twelve miles east of the state of New York, emissaries of General Washington made contact with the Comte de Rochambeau and called for the immediate assistance of the Duc de Lauzun. The American commander in chief wanted to surprise British and Hessian units foraging near Kingsbridge and asked that Lauzun's cavalry be dispatched with all possible speed to assist in the action, in cooperation with General Benjamin Lincoln's Continental regiments. Washington had an ambitious plan, but everything would depend on the results of the first engagements. If all went well at Kingsbridge, he hoped to build upon that initial success, penetrate more deeply into Manhattan and recapture Fort Washington and Harlem Heights.

Lauzun's cavalry was promptly sent south to cooperate with the Americans, while the main French army continued its march into Westchester County. The duke made a strong effort to support Washington's plan but arrived at Kingsbridge too late for effective coordinated action against the British and the Hessians. Even if Lauzun's horsemen had arrived on time, however, it probably would have made little difference. An American column had engaged a British foraging party prematurely, losing the element of surprise. The foragers quickly "retired within their strong works," and their rear guard put up an able defense.[187] The strike on the British outposts fell far short of its objective. The Americans and the Hessians had a firefight, and casualties were sustained on both sides. In his journal of the American war, Baron von Closen, aide to General Rochambeau, reported that the Hessian Jaegers killed or wounded thirty Americans.[188] This is how Washington explained the events at Kingsbridge in his diary entry for July 3:

> *The length of Duke Lauzun's March and the fatigue of his Corps prevented his coming to the point of Action at the hour appointed. In the meantime General Lincoln's party were attacked by the Yagers. Being disappointed in both objects from the causes mentioned, I did not care to fatigue the Troops any more but suffered them to remain on their arms while I spent a good part of the day in reconnoitering the Enemy's works.*[189]

THE FIFTH INDEPENDENCE DAY

The commander in chief then ordered the Continental army to withdraw twelve miles to the north, where it "took a position a little to the left of Dobbs ferry" and began to set up the American camps from the Hudson River eastward as far as Sprain Brook.[190] The first day of the Lower Westchester Encampment, July 4, 1781, was the fifth Independence Day of the United States. The significance of the anniversary was not lost on the men of the Continental army; they chose "Independence" as the password for the day. Their countersigns were "America" and "Glorious."[191]

Rochambeau's four infantry regiments had not yet arrived, and Washington utilized the time to designate a place for their campsites. He decided that the Sprain Brook, running north and south, would serve as the principal demarcation line between the two armies. The Americans would keep to the west of the Sprain and the French to the east. Washington's instructions to the quartermaster were explicit: "Take particular care that no house on the other side of the Wood and stream of Water on the left of the encampment are taken up for officers of the American Army; all on that side are to be appropriated to the officers of the French Army."[192]

The French Complete their March to the Encampment Site

By July 3, Rochambeau's troops had entered North Castle (today's Mount Kisco) in the northern part of Westchester County. From there, marching almost due south, they trod the final few miles of their 220-mile journey, and as they did, French officer and memoirist Clermont-Crèvecoeur took in the devastation around him: "Casting your eyes over the countryside, you felt very sad, for it revealed all the horrors and cruelty of the English in burned woodlands, destroyed houses, and fallow fields deserted by the owners."[193]

Baron von Closen's journal recorded that Westchester was oppressively hot on July 6, the final day of the French march. The troops suffered greatly because of the heat. Many couldn't keep up, and there were hundreds of stragglers. The baron reported that five French soldiers capitalized on the disorder to disappear into the woods:

> *The army left behind more than 400 stragglers, but they all rejoined us during the night, with the exception of two men from the Bourbonnais and three from the Deux-Ponts, who decided in favor of deserting to the woods, where they found shelter. Those from the Deux-Ponts were brought back, some days later, by some Americans,* good Whigs, *and were flogged.*[194]

It had been a difficult journey for the French army, especially on the final day. Yet they had made good time, covering 220 miles in just eleven days.

The 4,500 Continental troops and their 5,000 French allies established campsites side by side with astonishing expedition. By July 7, they were ready for "reciprocal visits by the two army corps."[195] French Ambassador de la Luzerne arrived in camp on that same date. On July 8 and 9, there were ceremonial presentations of arms and reviews by the commanding generals.

WHERE WERE THE AMERICAN AND FRENCH UNITS DEPLOYED AT THE ENCAMPMENT?

The American and French camps occupied the hilltops over an expanse of about ten miles, extending from Dobbs Ferry on the Hudson River eastward into present-day Ardsley, Hartsdale, Edgemont and White Plains. The Americans were deployed almost entirely to the west of the Sprain Brook and the French to the east. Amidst the French encampment, however, was an American unit commanded by Colonel David Waterbury and stationed to the east of the Bronx River, near the present-day border of Scarsdale and White Plains. Since the American and French armies were facing the powerful British forces of General Sir Henry Clinton in Manhattan to the south, we can speak of the American right and left and the French right and left, where right means west and left means east.

The Washington-Rochambeau Monument in Dobbs Ferry, commemorating the allied encampment of July and August 1781. *Author's photo.*

125

Most of the American units bivouacked in the northern part of present-day Ardsley, on either side of Heatherdell Road, a thoroughfare that existed in 1781 under a different name. Heatherdell Road was then a section of the "Dobbs ferry road,"[196] so named because it took travelers from White Plains, the county seat and commercial center, to the Dobbs's ferry landing for journeys across the Hudson.

Six years before, in September 1775, when John Adams traveled from his home in Braintree, Massachusetts, to Philadelphia to serve as a Massachusetts delegate to the Continental Congress, he passed along the Dobbs ferry road. We know this because he recorded each stop along his route, as well as all of his expenses. At Dobbs Ferry, he noted a payment of four shillings for "Dinners and Ferryage."[197] (Adams eventually submitted the account to the province of Massachusetts for reimbursement.)

Two months later, in November 1775, Martha Washington took the same route across Westchester County—but in the opposite direction— when she traveled from her home in Mount Vernon, Virginia, to join her husband in Massachusetts. General Washington had assumed command of the American army in Cambridge five months earlier.[198]

The old Dobbs ferry road—including the segment that we now know as Heatherdell Road—was one of the principal east–west crosscuts in Westchester County during the Revolutionary era. In addition to Heatherdell Road, other parts of the old Dobbs ferry road included today's Ashford Avenue in Dobbs Ferry, Ridge Road and Washington Avenue in present-day Hartsdale and Battle Road in White Plains.

General Washington made the Joseph Appleby House his headquarters, in present-day Hartsdale, about a half mile north of the old Dobbs ferry road (the part we now call Heatherdell Road) and a few yards north of the Hartsdale-Ardsley border, near the summit of a small hill, still known by old-timers in the community as Washington's Hill.[199] The Appleby House no longer stands.

About a mile to the east, General Rochambeau occupied the house of the widow Bates and made it his headquarters. It is known today as the Odell House because, after the Revolutionary War, it was purchased by the renowned Westchester Guide John Odell and remained in the Odell family through succeeding generations. It still stands on the north side of

Odell House on Ridge Road in Hartsdale. This was Rochambeau's headquarters in July and August 1781. View from the east. *Author's photo*.

Odell House on Ridge Road: view from the south. *Author's photo*.

the old Dobbs Ferry Road (the part we now call Ridge Road) in present-day Hartsdale. At the outbreak of the war, Odell was nineteen years old and most likely resided in his father Jonathan's home (the Harmse-Odell House) in present-day Irvington.[200]

Historian Robert Selig described the French campsites in his 2001 study of the Washington-Rochambeau Revolutionary Route in New York and identified the Sunningdale Country Club and Hart's Brook Nature Preserve and Arboretum as the corresponding modern-day locations.[201]

GEOGRAPHIC SYMMETRY

There was a geographic symmetry in the deployment of the allied forces. The American and French lines, labeled 1 and 2 on Captain Louis-Alexandre Berthier's map, were encamped on hilltops at the geographic

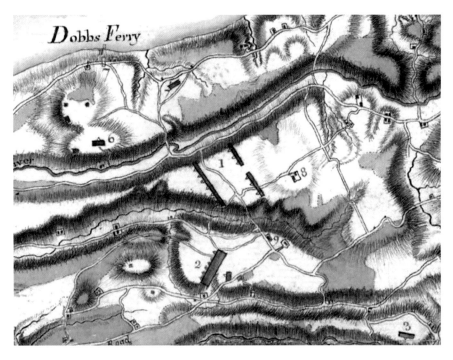

Map of the Lower Westchester Encampment, drawn in 1781 by French officer Louis-Alexandre Berthier. Detail from Position du camp de l'armée combinée a Philipsburg. *Rochambeau Map Collection, Library of Congress.*

center, while elite units were positioned about two miles away, at locations of maximum vulnerability, to provide protection and early warning to the center. On the French side, White Plains was the most exposed location, since all main roads converged there. If the British were to attack from Long Island Sound, they would probably land in the vicinity of Mamaroneck and advance first on White Plains. Hence, French elite units—the chasseurs (light infantry), the grenadiers and the Legion de Lauzun (a mixed force, including cavalry)—were posted in White Plains, two miles to the northeast of the French line.

The American elite units, Scammel's light infantry and Sheldon's dragoons, were encamped two miles to the southwest of the American line, in Dobbs Ferry, the most exposed point on the right because of its location on the Hudson River. It was reasonable to expect that a British offensive against the encampment would come from the Hudson, and that was, in fact, exactly what happened. During the six and a half weeks of the encampment, the only strikes against it were made by British raiding vessels on the Hudson River.

Scammel's camp was sometimes simply called the "light camp," to contrast it with the main American camp in northern Ardsley. Lieutenant Colonel Alexander Hamilton was stationed with Scammel, and when Hamilton wrote letters to his new bride (he had married Elizabeth Schuyler in December 1780), he put the place name "light camp" at the top of his letters.

Scammel's light infantry occupied the high ground in eastern Dobbs Ferry, the site of Children's Village today. Colonel Sheldon's dragoons were positioned farther to the right, on the high ground known as Villard Hill today, and at the Dobbs Ferry redoubt, which was located on the steep slope rising from the Hudson and therefore gave an excellent view of the river.[202] What appear to be remnants of the Dobbs Ferry redoubt still overlook the Hudson today, at the intersection of Broadway and Livingston Avenue. Berthier's map shows Sheldon's dragoons (labeled 7) in two locations along the river road (today's Broadway) in Dobbs Ferry.

Louis-Alexandre Berthier

At the time of the encampment, Louis-Alexandre Berthier was a twenty-eight-year-old captain in Rochambeau's army and an assistant quartermaster general. This meant that it was his job to range widely through the southern part of Westchester County at the head of large French foraging parties. In the journal that he kept, Berthier explains:

> *Being definitely on the edge of enemy territory, the army was ordered to forage in advance of the position, as close to the enemy as possible. The assistant quartermasters-general were continually employed in reconnoitering forage…these foraging expeditions covered an area between the camp and Long Island Sound, extending from Rye, Mamaroneck, East Chester, and Chester to a point as close as possible to King's Bridge…I took advantage of these foraging expeditions…to make a survey of the country.*

Berthier prepared many maps for General Rochambeau, drawing rivers, roads and topographical features in effusive detail, from Rhode Island to Virginia. Much of the information that we now have about the Washington-Rochambeau Revolutionary Route is derived from

---

**Key for 1781 encampment sites
on both modern map and original map**

1. Main American camp
2. Main French camp
3. Grenadiers & chasseurs (French light infantry)
4. Legion of Lauzun
5. Corps of Col. Waterbury
6. Corps of Col. Scammel (American light infantry)
7. Sheldon's dragoons
8. Headquarters of Gen. Washington
9. Headquarters of Gen. Rochambeau
10. French hospital
11. Batteries at Dobbs Ferry to prevent ships from coming up the river

---

this astonishing cartographical opus. In his journal, as in his maps, he displays his appreciation of topography. "The American army," he writes, describing the Lower Westchester Encampment sites, "composed the right wing, resting on the Saw Mill River to which you descend by a steep bluff; the American artillery park occupied the center." Berthier continues:

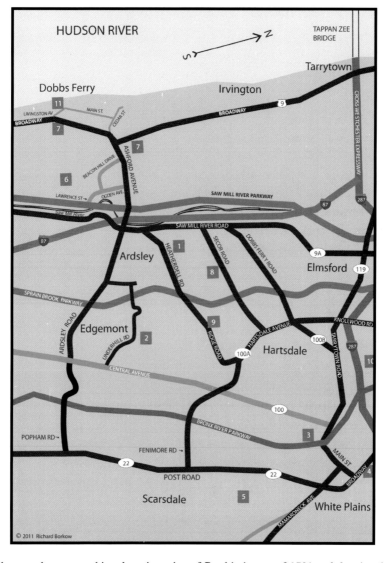

Modern road map, matching the orientation of Berthier's map of 1781 and showing the 1781 encampment sites.

The American light infantry and dragoons were strung out from the right of the line all the way to Dobbs Ferry on the Hudson River, where a battery of four 12-pounders and two howitzers was emplaced.

The French composed the left wing, resting on the Bronx River, whose banks are very steep... The heights at the left of the line were occupied by the French grenadiers and chasseurs [and] the Lauzun Legion...

The field pieces were laid before the camp at each opening in the front of attack. The main guards were posted in advance on the most strategic heights, guarding all points at which the enemy could approach the camp.[203]

The British Attack Supply Boats at Tarrytown

General Sir Henry Clinton proceeded cautiously. Convinced that Manhattan was the sole objective of the allies, he felt that a defensive policy would be his best option. But he did not remain totally cocooned on his well-defended island; instead, he sent warships up the Hudson to test allied defenses at Dobbs Ferry and to interrupt supplies that were coming down the river.

The British made their strongest move against the allied encampment on July 15. On that date, under cover of darkness, King George's ships sailed north up the Hudson past Dobbs Ferry, where batteries had been erected on both the eastern and western shores. "In defiance of [the] cannon" at Dobbs Ferry, the warships continued north and entered the Tappan Zee.

Near Tarrytown, the British warships came upon American supply boats with ordnance and bread for the allied armies. The supply boats scurried for safe berth at Tarrytown and ran aground there. Colonel Sheldon and his dragoons, stationed at Dobbs Ferry and aware of the threat to the supply boats, quickly marched to their defense:

Col. Sheldon (whose regiment lay at Dobb's Ferry) immediately marched his mounted dragoons to the place, where he ordered his men to dismount and assist to unload the stores, which was done with great despatch. By this time the enemy having come to anchor off Tarrytown, began a heavy cannonade, under cover of which they sent two gunboats and four barges to destroy the vessels. [204]

In the action that followed, we can see the determination and the mettle of Sheldon's dragoons:

Captain Hurlbert, of the second regiment of light dragoons, was stationed on board one of [the vessels] *with 12 men,…finding himself surrounded,* [he] *ordered his men to jump overboard and make for the shore, which they did, he following; the enemy immediately boarded and set fire to the vessels, but were obliged immediately to retire, owing to the severe fire that was kept up by the dragoons and French guard. Capt. Hurlbert, Capt.-Lieut. Miles, Quartermaster Shaylor, and others, jumped into the river and made for the* [supply boats], *in order to extinguish the fire, which they did, and saved the vessels; while in the water, Capt. H. received a musket ball through the thigh, but is now in a fair way to do well.* [205]

General Washington issued a statement of commendation on July 19: "The commander-in-chief is exceedingly pleased with…the gallant behavior and spirited exertions of Colonel Sheldon and Captain Hurlbert, of the second regiment of dragoons;…[their] preserving the whole of the ordnance and stores from destruction, entitle them to the most distinguished notice and applause of their general." [206]

EXCHANGE OF CANNON FIRE AT THE DOBBS FERRY REDOUBT

The British warships had failed in their attempt to disrupt supplies. They now had the problem of returning from the Tappan Zee to safety in New York Harbor. To do so, they would have to run the gauntlet again at Dobbs Ferry. The British ships had passed by the Dobbs Ferry batteries unscathed on July 15. But on the return trip (July 19), the largest and most imposing of the British vessels, the HMS *Savage*, sustained significant damage.

Thacher's description follows:

[July] *19th,—the British frigates that passed up the North River a few days since, took the advantage of wind and tide to return to New York. A severe cannonade commenced from our battery at Dobbs' ferry, where the river is about 3 miles wide, and they were compelled to run the gauntlet. They returned to the fire as they passed, but without effect. On board the Savage ship of war a box of powder took fire, and such was their consternation, that 20 people jumped into the river; among whom was a prisoner on board, who informs us that he was the only man who got on shore, all of the others being drowned. He reports also that the Savage was several times hulled by our shot, and was very near sinking.*[207]

The site of the Dobbs Ferry redoubt at the corner of Broadway and Livingston Avenue. View from sidewalk. *Author's photo.*

The site of the Dobbs Ferry redoubt at the corner of Broadway and Livingston Avenue. View from vest-pocket park. *Author's photo.*

Stone marker in the vest-pocket park. The original site of this marker was about 150 yards north, implying the presence of more than one redoubt in 1781. *Author's photo.*

Redoubt, Dobbs Ferry, Jasper F. Cropsey, 1892. *Collection of the Newington-Cropsey Foundation.*

THE GRAND RECONNAISSANCE

In the most extensive reconnoitering mission, the so-called Grand Reconnaissance (July 21 to July 23), Washington and Rochambeau surveyed the northern line of British defenses from the west at Kingsbridge to the east, along the Harlem River as far as Long Island Sound. Since the allies were penetrating deeply into territories occupied since 1776 by armed British sympathizers, the operation was, of necessity, a reconnaissance in force, and there was active skirmishing with Tory guerillas. The allies emerged the victors in these encounters, for the Loyalist militiamen were no match for regular troops.

The principal clash with Tory guerrillas occurred on the shores of the Harlem River, at Morrisania, named for the Morris half brothers, Lewis and Gouverneur, both Patriot leaders.[208] When the British occupied Manhattan in 1776, Lewis Morris had been forced to abandon his home and holdings along the Harlem River, and the property had become the headquarters of Loyalist leader James Delancey.

Some twenty British sympathizers, from their place of refuge in a house on the Morris estate, directed musket fire at the approaching French and American regulars, one of whom was Captain Louis-Alexandre Berthier.

According to Berthier's account, the house was soon surrounded, and the men inside announced that they would surrender. But when the group exited the building, they noticed about two hundred Loyalist confederates across the river, concluded that the tables had turned and thought better of their decision to surrender. The group started to charge the regulars, firing muskets at them and even field pieces loaded with grapeshot. Berthier recounts what happened when a Loyalist with a pistol in each hand rushed at him, blasting away with one of his pistols: "He fired at me at 5 paces, grazing my ear, and crying, 'Die, you dog of a Frenchman.' He was about to fire his other [pistol] when I got ahead of him and put a ball through his chest, which killed him on the spot. We sabered, shot or captured the rest...captured 10 men and 7 horses. The rest flung themselves into the river, where some of them perished."[209]

The larger purpose of the Grand Reconnaissance was to uncover vulnerabilities in the British line of defense along its northern perimeter. As the expedition moved west to east, from Spuyten Duyvil Creek to the Harlem River, Washington carefully studied the Manhattan shoreline, searching for possible landing sites for an invading force. Just to the west of Kingsbridge, he noted that "the Fort on Cox's Hill was in bad repair... there is neither ditch nor friezing to it, and the No. East Corner appears quite easy of access...The approach to the inner Point...is secured by a ledge of Rocks which would conceal a party from observation."[210]

That was not the only promising site. An incursion against Manhattan might be launched from the Hudson River as well. A week before, on July 18, Washington had "passed the North River with Count de Rochambeau" to inspect British defenses from the New Jersey side.[211] Studying Manhattan island from across the river, he observed that "there seems to be a place [near Fort Knyphausen]...which has the best appearance of landing, and is most private."[212]

Washington concluded that the Manhattan shoreline had vulnerabilities. An invasion might be successful—but only if the allies had sufficient numbers of men. To defeat the British and Hessian armies, even to gain a foothold, the invaders must attack in sufficient strength. It was a well-known principle of war that an attacking force would have little chance of success against a fortified position unless the invaders greatly outnumbered the defenders; some said the ratio must be two or three to one.

De Grasse's ships might arrive in New York Harbor teeming with French infantry regiments to supplement the allied armies. But even if de Grasse could furnish an additional 3,000 men, it would not be enough to outnumber the defenders on Manhattan. To Washington's chagrin, the Continental battalions at the encampment were still embarrassingly undermanned. The commander in chief had assured Rochambeau at Wethersfield about troop levels "on the faith of the states," and the states were letting him down.

Chapter 8

GEORGE WASHINGTON'S WESTCHESTER GAMBLE

Washington's undectectably swift transfer of his forces from New York to Virginia was the largest and perhaps the boldest movement of the war.[213]
—Benson Bobrick

In the August 1 entry of his diary, Washington acknowledged that there was little reason to expect a successful attack against British New York: "Everything would have been in perfect readiness," he wrote, "to commence the operation against New York, if the States had furnished their quotas of men...but so far have they been from complying with these that...not more than half the number asked of them have joined the Army."[214] "Thus circumstanced...I could scarce see a ground upon wch. to continue my preparations against New York...and therefore I turned my views more seriously (than I had before done) to an operation to the Southward."[215]

Still, he wrote, it was possible that things could turn around. The states might yet honor their troop commitments.[216] And de Grasse might arrive, bringing thousands of additional soldiers on board his ships. Washington instructed General David Forman, stationed on the New Jersey coast at Monmouth, to be on the lookout for Admiral de Grasse's fleet and to set up a chain of speedy couriers from Monmouth to Dobbs Ferry to inform Washington immediately about the arrival of the French warships.[217]

The chain of couriers was a great expense that Washington could hardly afford, but that could not be helped: success in this campaign would depend upon speedy, reliable communication with Admiral de Grasse.

SUPERINTENDENT OF FINANCE ROBERT MORRIS

Robert Morris, one of the wealthiest men in the country and its first superintendent of finance, left Philadelphia on August 7 to begin a four-day trip across New Jersey in order to meet with General Washington at his camp by the Hudson. Morris had been appointed superintendent of finance just a few weeks before and accepted the job only after insisting that Congress grant him almost total independence in the operations of his office. By demanding a role that was independent of the legislators, Morris was essentially creating, for the first time, an executive branch of the United States government.

Accompanying Morris was Richard Peters, head of the Congress's Board of War.[218] Morris and Peters had an unpleasant assignment: they would have to inform Washington that army expenditures and manpower levels, restricted as they already were, would of necessity be reduced even further in 1782. They arrived on August 11 and, over the next several days, met frequently with Washington in order to work out the details of the new draconian budget (which the commander in chief stoutly resisted).

But on August 14, the fifth day of their discussions, a communication arrived at the Westchester camps that changed the course of the war. It forced Morris and Peters to drop their focus on 1782 and direct all of their attention, instead, to the campaign of 1781. The communication had been sent to Washington and Rochambeau by Admiral Barras in Newport, and it conveyed the intention of Admiral de Grasse to bring his fleet not to New York but rather to Virginia.

A WAKE-UP CALL AT REVEILLE

Decades later, Richard Peters recalled the circumstances early on the morning of August 14 when he and Robert Morris first learned from Washington about de Grasse's message:

One morning, at the beat of reveille, Mr. Morris and myself… were roused by a messenger from headquarters, and desired forthwith to repair thither…The General…the moment he saw me, with expressions of intemperate passion (which I will not repeat), handed me a letter from [Admiral de Barras], *who commanded six or seven ships at Rhode Island.*

"*Here,*" *said the general,* "*read this; you understand the French;*" *and, turning away,* "*so do I now better than ever*"…

Mr. M. and myself stood silent, and not a little astonished. The letter informed the General that [de Barras] *had received* [the news that] *de Grasse* [would bring his fleet to] *the Chesapeake…if anything could be done in the southern quarters, cooperation was offered* [to Generals Washington and Rochambeau] *during the few weeks of his intended stay in those waters, to avoid the West India hurricane season. Secrecy was enjoined, and we went our way.*

On returning to breakfast, we found that General as composed as if nothing extraordinary had happened…I had often (for I knew him from early life) admired these conquests over himself…In the course of the day I was asked by the General, "*well, what can you do for us, under the present change of circumstances?*"[219]

Washington's initial irritation was no doubt due to the summary cancellation of his plans and the sudden narrowing of his options. He had never ruled out an operation in the South. And he clearly recognized that his New York strategy was not going to work.

But he had requested, even if the allies were to turn to a southern operation, that de Grasse's fleet arrive first in New York Harbor. The American army could then, he hoped, be transported to Virginia aboard de Grasse's ships and the dangers associated with a long march avoided.

Between reveille and breakfast, Washington appears to have made his decision. When Peters saw him at breakfast, the general was composed and seemed at peace with the bold alteration in his plans. The New York operation would be abandoned. All efforts would be directed instead toward preparations for a march to the South.

SEA AND LAND MOVEMENTS WOULD HAVE TO BE COORDINATED PERFECTLY. NOTHING COULD GO WRONG.

To move the armies south more than four hundred miles would involve enormous risks. Success would require the precise coordination of multiple sea and land movements and would depend on unreliable communications at great distances. Success would also require the utmost secrecy. If Clinton were to learn about the change in plans, he could quickly dispatch his fleet to block de Grasse and de Barras. And he could warn Cornwallis, or rescue him, before the trap was set. Moreover, if Clinton became aware prematurely of the allies' new destination, he could easily obstruct their march, using his navy to disrupt them at their vulnerable Hudson River crossing or attacking their stretched-out and exposed lines at other vulnerable points along the route.

Marching the Continental army south would lead to additional perils. Washington had emphasized them at Wethersfield. The greatest concern was that the Continental troops would be reluctant to march to Virginia, a place they associated with swamp fevers and malaria. The problem, he felt, would be solved if the men were paid—and in specie this time, not with nearly worthless Continentals. But if they were not paid, Washington feared that many would not march at all and that large numbers would melt away as the army proceeded south.

Apart from the problem of the unpaid men, the scarcity of funds would undermine the march south for a host of other reasons. Horses and wagons could not be hired, and many would be needed for the trek. Boats to take the troops down the Chesapeake would not be available without money. It would even be difficult to procure basic provisions.

Then there were the naval dilemmas. They were mostly out of Washington's hands, but they would be worries, nonetheless. It was far from certain, first of all, that de Grasse's ships could actually gain control of Chesapeake Bay, for the British fleet would most likely present a vigorous challenge to him when he made the attempt. De Barras would face an even greater danger from King George's ships. After he left the relative security of Newport Harbor and brought his much weaker squadron into the open sea, he was at risk of annihilation by the British navy. Yet de Barras, who had the allies' only siege guns, would have to make his way safely into the Chesapeake Bay. An effective siege of Cornwallis would be inconceivable with those guns.

Moreover, de Grasse was insisting that he could remain in the Chesapeake Bay only until October 15, and this was of great concern. Two months were hardly enough time to do all that had to be done. The American and French armies would have to break camp and begin their march immediately, rush down to Virginia, set up the siege of Cornwallis (if he still happened to be on the coast when they arrived) and maintain it for an unknown number of days.[220]

Perhaps the near abandonment of the Hudson Highlands and West Point would be the greatest gamble of all. Washington and the Continental army had protected them for years. If the allied armies actually left the Hudson region, those invaluable assets would be imperiled. A march to Virginia would compel Washington to take much of his army south, leaving a mere skeleton force to protect the post at West Point. To counter the move of the allies to the south, might not Clinton advance on West Point and overwhelm its few defenders? Washington and Rochambeau might find, when they got to Virginia, not only that Cornwallis had slipped away and was safe in the Carolinas but that West Point had also been lost. Would it not be better just to stay in place and not take such an enormous risk?

Washington Gambles Everything on a March South

Washington was a proven risk taker. Under desperate circumstances, he had chanced the survival of his army to cross the Delaware and attack the Hessians at Trenton on Christmas 1776. In 1779, to answer Clinton's punishing raids against Westchester and the Connecticut coast, he had sent Anthony Wayne on a perilous mission to seize Stony Point.

It was a time for audacity again. The commander in chief wrote on August 14, 1781, that he would march to Virginia "for the purpose of cooperating with [de Grasse's] force…against the [British] Troops in that state":

14th…Matters having now come to a crisis and a decisive plan to be determined on, I was obliged, from the shortness of Count de Grasse's promised stay on this Coast, the apparent disinclination in their Naval Officers to force the harbour of New York and the feeble compliance of the States to my requisitions for Men, hitherto, and little prospect of greater exertion in the future, to give up all idea of attacking New York; and instead thereof to remove the French Troops and a detachment from the American Army to the Head of Elk, to be transported to Virginia for the purpose of co-operating with the force from the West Indies against the Troops in that State.[221]

The next day, Washington wrote to Lafayette, explaining the radical change of strategy. Count de Grasse's destination is the Chesapeake, he told the young general, and he will bring between twenty-five and twenty-nine ships of the line and a considerable body of land forces. Look for him every moment! Cornwallis will no doubt try to escape from "so formidable an armament" and retreat into North Carolina. Do everything you can to prevent it! In the letter, Washington intimated, without being explicit, that Lafayette would be receiving "aid from this quarter."[222]

Plans for the march were urgently formulated over the next five days. Only a few senior officers were aware that the army's destination would be Virginia. The American commander in chief decided that the armies would cross the Hudson River at Kings Ferry, twenty miles north of Dobbs Ferry—and twenty miles farther from the British fleet in New York Harbor.

The Continental army would march along the river road (Broadway) moving north through present-day Irvington and the villages of Tarrytown and Sing Sing (Ossining). The French army would take a separate route to the north, along the interior roads of Westchester County, eventually passing through Peekskill and then dropping a few miles south from that village to Kings Ferry. On Sunday, August 19, the Continental army broke camp in Dobbs Ferry and present-day Ardsley to begin the march. The French army broke camp on the same date about three miles to the east of Dobbs Ferry.

Early that Sunday morning, the American units coming out of Ardsley and Scammel's light infantry regiment, coming from the hills of eastern Dobbs Ferry, assembled together ("were paraded for the march") at the intersection of the river road (Broadway today) and the old Dobbs Ferry

Road (Ashford Avenue).[223] Today the intersection is known as Dobbs Ferry's Gateway. There, Scammel's men were probably placed at the head of the American army, for his light infantry regiment ordinarily marched in the van.[224]

The American troops assumed that they would be instructed to turn left at the Gateway intersection and march south toward Kingsbridge,

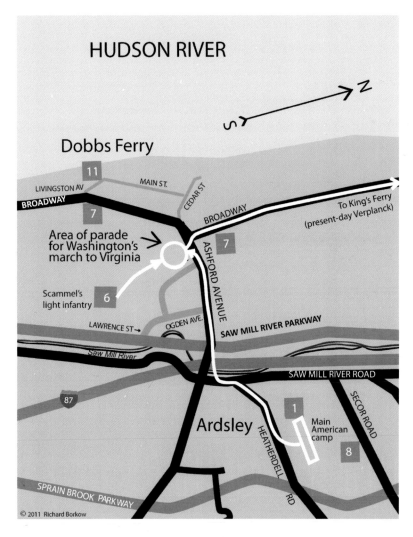

Modern road map showing area of the parade for Washington's march to Virginia, August 19, 1781.

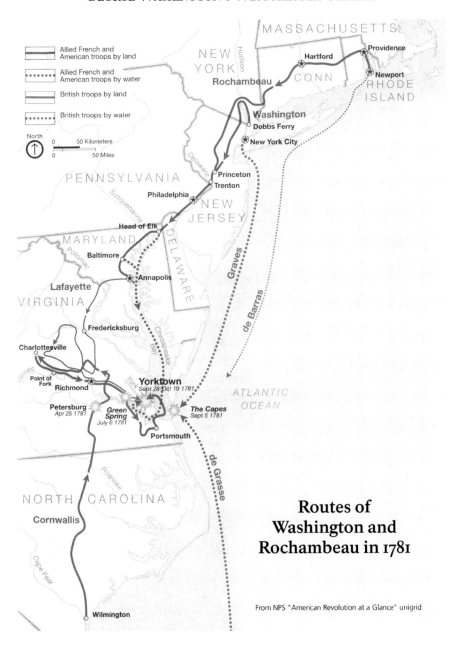

Map of Washington's march to Virginia. *National Park Service: American Revolution at a Glance, 2001. www.nps.gov/carto/PDF/AMREAmap7.pdf.*

since the road toward Kingsbridge had been cleared and since they had been instructed to march that way more than once before. Thus, they were puzzled by the orders that were actually issued: to turn right, not left, and to march north. Dr. Thacher's journal entry for August 20, 1781, explains:

> *August 20th. 1781—According to orders, we commenced our line of march yesterday, a party of pioneers being sent forward to clear the road towards King's-bridge, and we expected immediately to follow in that direction; but an army is a machine, whose motions are directed by its chief. When the troops were paraded for the march, they were ordered to the right about, and, making a retrograde movement up the side of the North river, we have reached King's-ferry* [at Verplanck], *and are preparing to cross the Hudson at this ferry.*[225]

Historian Benson Bobrick calls Washington's march from the Hudson to Virginia "the largest and perhaps boldest movement of the war."[226] Since it led to the Franco-American victory at Yorktown, it was also the most consequential movement of the war. Recent interest in key sites along the Washington-Rochambeau Trail has focused attention on the Gateway intersection, where the men were paraded, since a parade for the march preceded any major movement of the army.

THE MARCH FROM THE HUDSON TO VIRGINIA

Historian H.J. Eckenrode, writing in 1931, speculates on the reasons for the success of the march: "Probably the movement against Yorktown succeeded because of its very boldness. Probably Sir Henry Clinton did not believe that Washington would leave New York and New Jersey practically defenseless while he carried the French and American armies to Chesapeake Bay."[227]

The passage of the Americans and the French across the Hudson River at Kings Ferry took four days to complete. During the crossing, they were exposed and vulnerable, and there was plenty of time for Clinton to react. If the allies had been attacked by his warships, there would have been few options available for defense. Where, then, was the British fleet?[228]

Count Deux-Ponts expressed his astonishment that the British did not try to interrupt the crossing: "An enemy of any boldness or any skill would have seized an opportunity so favorable for him and so embarrassing for us...I do not understand the indifference with which Gen. Clinton considers our movements. It is to me an obscure enigma."[229]

After the allied armies arrived at Stony Point on the western side of the river, they started to march south, in the direction of Virginia. But they were also marching toward Staten Island, an important British outpost that defended Clinton's Manhattan stronghold. Because of the geographic good fortune that Staten Island was many miles south, Washington's campaign of deception could continue for several days, until the armies arrived in the region of New Jersey opposite that British outpost. Washington then made a feint toward Staten Island, and one regiment pretended to build artillery batteries, as if planning an attack.[230] Clinton responded by concentrating troops on Staten Island, ready to meet the allied attack and defend his post.[231] The American commander had already made other efforts to keep the ruse going by ordering the conspicuous construction of large bread ovens on the New Jersey side of the river, as if the two armies were planning a long stay, as they would for a siege. Clinton remained convinced that he was the target of the allied maneuvers, until the truth dawned early in September.

The unpaid men continued to march, but there were rumblings of discontent.[232] Finally, when the two armies arrived in Philadelphia, Washington quickly renewed contact with Robert Morris, who had left the encampment for the capital on August 18. What, Washington asked, could be done to pay the men? By a stroke of fortune, John Laurens appeared in Philadelphia at precisely this time to assure Washington and Morris that he had just disembarked in Boston with the six million livres donated by France and that the money would soon arrive in Philadelphia. Laurens's report gave a boost to American credit, making it easier to borrow funds. Morris himself made a large monetary contribution, dipping deeply into his own personal accounts.[233] The men received their pay south of Philadelphia, at Head of Elk (at the northern tip of the Chesapeake Bay). It was hard money, not paper, and it brought the rumblings to an end. Some of the soldiers commented that it was the first time they had ever received their payment in the form of specie.

The next requirement was the safe arrival, in the Chesapeake Bay, of Admirals de Grasse and de Barras. The allied generals were south of Philadelphia when they received the first updates on the whereabouts of de Grasse. Rochambeau and other French officers were sailing down the Delaware River past Chester, Pennsylvania, when they noticed a jumping figure on the shore who was vigorously waving his hat. Was that the sedate and reserved General Washington? Unbelievably, it was. The French officers brought the ship to shore, and there an ecstatic Washington embraced Rochambeau, telling him the news: de Grasse had not only entered Chesapeake Bay with twenty-nine ships of the line but had also brought 3,500 French troops with him, who had already disembarked at Jamestown Island, near Williamsburg.

SEPTEMBER 5, 1781: THE SECOND BATTLE OF THE CAPES

De Grasse's armada was in possession of the Chesapeake Bay, at least for the time being. The unresolved question was whether he could maintain control, for the British were sure to confront him. By late August, Admiral Thomas Graves, commander of the British fleet in New York, was aware that de Grasse had left the West Indies and suspected that he was headed to North America to give aid to Washington and Rochambeau. Hoping to locate de Grasse's fleet and put it out of commission, Graves left New York Harbor on September 1. When he departed New York, Admiral Graves, like Sir Henry Clinton, had no idea that Cornwallis was in danger. Both still believed that Washington and Rochambeau were intending to besiege New York.

British Admiral George Rodney, active in the West Indies that summer, would have given de Grasse a real challenge. He was a creative tactician and a very aggressive commander, who outranked Graves and had the right to assume command of Graves's New York fleet. But in the first week of September, when the French and British fleets fought the second Battle of the Capes, Rodney was on his way back to England, explaining that he needed to return home because he was ill. Some believed that the real reason for his return home was his need to manage the vast piles of booty that he had acquired from his conquest of the rich West Indian island of Stacia in February 1781. Whatever the reason for Rodney's absence, Thomas Graves, a hesitant and unimaginative tactician, whose capabilities in command were very much inferior to those of Rodney, would be the man in charge of the British fleet at the second Battle of the Capes.

Because of faulty intelligence from the West Indies, Graves, sailing south from New York with nineteen ships of the line, expected that de Grasse would have only fourteen of the monster warships. He was no doubt dismayed when he arrived at the Capes to find the French admiral inside Chesapeake Bay with more than twenty.[234] Nevertheless, even though de Grasse had a numerical edge, the winds were blowing from the northeast, giving Graves, who was also coming from the north and the east, a strong advantage. To get out of the bay and into the Atlantic, the French warships had to tack against the wind and were forced to move laboriously and unevenly. A large gap developed between the van and the center of the French line.

This was the time to strike. The British could have concentrated their cannon fire on de Grasse's isolated van, which consisted of only three or four vessels, and destroyed them all. But Graves waited more than an hour while the gap closed. His failure to act has puzzled military historians ever since. It was only the first of his blunders. During the battle, Graves's flagship flew contradictory signals simultaneously; when he gave a new order to close on the enemy, which would require the British ships to move south, he forgot to take down the signal to move east, causing great confusion.

When the British and French fleets did engage in late afternoon, both suffered damage and casualties, and the British got the worst of it by far. The fleets then drifted south for several days, ending up opposite Cape Hatteras. Remarkably, Admiral de Barras, with his relatively weak squadron of six ships of the line, arrived at the Capes exactly when Graves and de Grasse were drifting south, and he slipped unnoticed and unhindered into Chesapeake Bay, conveying the essential siege guns. If Graves had seen de Barras before the Battle of the Capes, the small

French flotilla would have been easy prey. De Barras most likely would have been trounced and the siege guns sunk to the bottom of the Atlantic.

The second Battle of the Capes all but determined the fate of Cornwallis at Yorktown. Graves's fleet was so badly damaged that it was forced to return to New York for repairs, and de Grasse reentered Chesapeake Bay unopposed around September 10, where he was delighted to find de Barras. The combined French strength in the bay was now thirty-four ships of the line.

THE FATE OF THE AMERICAN REPUBLIC WAS DECIDED ON THE SEAS
Britain had reason to feel secure about the strength of its fleet after its astonishing naval victories during the French and Indian War (1755 to 1763), especially in the *annus mirabilis* of 1759. But one wonders whether the British sense of security and conviction of dominance may have led to overconfidence and miscalculation by the time of the Revolutionary War. King George's navy had a significant problem of leadership, and Great Britain could not take for granted either superior central command or superior admiralship. Military historians have judged the Earl of Sandwich, Lord of the Admiralty, to have been a highly incompetent minister. Under his lackluster direction, the Admiralty became careless about the maintenance of its fleet and the quality of its admirals. Considering how great was Great Britain's dependency on naval power, these errors had serious consequences in the summer of 1781.

The fate of the American republic was decided on the seas. John Adams, Benjamin Franklin and Charles Vergennes always presumed that the outcome of the war would be determined by naval power, as did Generals Washington and Rochambeau. Understanding how critical naval power would be, France made an extraordinary effort to achieve naval dominance in the North American theater. There were several major disappointments at first, and naval dominance was not easily achieved. But in the end, France's effort paid off. And because it did, the United States won its independence.

YORKTOWN

When Cornwallis understood the "formidable armament" that was being assembled against him, he considered the option of forcing his way out of Yorktown. However, the strength of the land armies that would oppose him had grown considerably, even before Washington and Rochambeau arrived on the scene. By mid-September, there were about seven thousand American and French soldiers in proximity to Yorktown who would have been potentially available to resist any breakout by Cornwallis.[235]

And there was another factor: Clinton began to send Cornwallis messages of encouragement from New York. The letters came at night on small boats captained by brave men who managed to elude the huge French warships. On September 28, Cornwallis received a letter from Clinton, dated September 24, with a reassuring promise: "At a meeting of the general and flag officers held this day, it is determined, that above 5000 men…shall be embarked…in a few days to relieve you."[236]

In the letter of September 24, Clinton told Cornwallis that twenty-three ships would come from New York to assist in the rescue.[237] The effect of the letters was to encourage Cornwallis to stay in place and reject proposals suggested by others (notably Banastre Tarleton) to risk a breakout attempt.

The American and French armies arrived from the North in staggered fashion. Some came by boat down the Chesapeake Bay, and some traveled overland. By late September, most of the 7,500 men who had marched from the encampment by the Hudson were in Williamsburg, which served as the staging area for the Yorktown siege. The British had also fortified Gloucester across from Yorktown on the north side of the York River, and the encirclement would include Gloucester as well.

The siege had a preparatory phase that lasted almost two weeks, from September 28 to October 9. During those two weeks, trenches were dug for placement of the French and American artillery. Some of the big French guns had been manufactured according to the system of General Gribeauval, a technological innovator, whose artillery was the most advanced in the world.[238] Gribeauval's large cannon, apparently first employed in combat on the battlefield at Yorktown, were extremely accurate. Washington marveled at the capability of the weapons, which would eventually give Napoleon a technological edge and contribute to his conquests in Europe. The second phase of the siege of Yorktown began on October 9 with the bombardment of the British works. On the night of October 16, the British and Hessian army made a desperate attempt to escape by boat across the York River to Gloucester. From there they hoped to break through the ring encircling them on the north. The bold attempt failed, not because it was thwarted by the allies but because of an intense storm that made the river crossing impossible.

COLONEL SCAMMEL AT YORKTOWN

Colonel Alexander Scammel was at the Battle of Yorktown, but he did not survive it. He received a mortal gun wound while reconnoitering close to British entrenchments. He lingered for six days, and Dr. Thacher, who apparently had the opportunity to speak with him during those final days, reported that the shooting of Scammel occurred after he had surrendered. It was concluded that Scammel had been denied the rights and protections due a prisoner of war.

The death of the extremely popular Scammel came as a hard blow to the American army. The American soldiers were especially outraged by the report that Scammel was not given quarter after he had tried to surrender. Following Cornwallis's surrender, Scammel was buried with honor at Williamsburg, and a monument was placed over his grave with this inscription:

> *Which conquering armies from their toils returned,*
> *Rear to his glory, while his fate they mourned.*

CORNWALLIS SURRENDERS

On October 19, 1781, two months to the day following the departure of the Continental army from Dobbs Ferry, Cornwallis surrendered his entire army, consisting of about 7,500 British and Hessian troops, to the allied American and French forces. The allied armies totaled about 16,600, comprising 8,800 American and 7,800 French troops.[239]

EPILOGUE

King George and his ministers were completely unprepared for the reports of Cornwallis's surrender at Yorktown. The American and French armies had moved south and won their victory at Yorktown so quickly that London was not even aware that Cornwallis had been in danger.[240]

Lord North, the prime minister, responded to the news as if he had suffered a physical blow. "And how did [Lord North] take it?" was the inquiry to George Germain. "As he would have taken a ball in the breast," replied Lord George, "for he opened his arms, exclaiming wildly as he paced up and down the apartment, 'Oh God! It is all over!'"[241] The vehemence of his reaction aside, Lord North's forecast was, of course, on target. A practical man, and not a hardliner, he immediately understood the political ramifications of the British debacle in Virginia.

The response of the hardliners, most notably the king, George Germain and a small coterie of other ministers, took a different form. Great Britain still controlled the major port cities of New York, Charleston and Savannah. Why should those important posts be given up? By altering its military strategy, Britain would be able to absorb the reversal at Yorktown. It had done so after Saratoga and had been able to carry on the war for four years. It could accommodate again.

In Parliamentary debate in December, weeks after the news from Yorktown had been received, Germain seemed not to have budged at all from his hardline position. "The moment that the House [of Commons] recognized the independence of America," he declared, "the British empire was ruined."[242]

This was the king's policy as well. Lord North, however, was more realistic. During all the years of the war, he had been able to maintain large majorities in Parliament to sustain the war effort, despite the strong criticism that was voiced eloquently and repeatedly by the greatest Parliamentary orators of the day, William Pitt and Edmund Burke.

Cornwallis's defeat, Lord North realized, was not being viewed by the members of Parliament as an ordinary military setback. In the context of the long, costly war, they regarded his capitulation to Washington and Rochambeau as a major reversal. For the first time, Parliamentary support for the war was seriously at risk.

The prime minister was an expert at counting votes, and his forecast was correct. Parliamentary support for the war was doomed. But the process proved to be slow, and the road to peace would be a long one; a year and a half would pass before a peace treaty was ratified both by Congress and by Parliament.

THE KING'S LETTER OF ABDICATION

The faction opposed to the war in the House of Commons increased its strength only by degrees, and it would take four months before the Lord North–George Germain government fell from power. Finally, in mid-March 1782, a no-confidence vote became inevitable. From the viewpoint of King George, it was the worst week of his reign. He saw no choice but to write a letter of abdication. In his own hand he penned the following:

> *His Majesty is convinced that the sudden change of the Sentiments of one branch of the Legislature has totally incapacitated Him from either conducting the War with effect, or from obtaining any Peace but on conditions which would prove destructive to the Commerce as well as the essential Rights of the British Nation.*

His Majesty therefore with much sorrow finds He can be of no further Utility to his Native Country which drives him to the painful step of quitting it forever.

In consequence of which Intention his Majesty resigns the Crown of Great Britain and the Dominions appertaining thereto to His Dearly Beloved Son and lawful Successor, George Prince of Wales, whose endeavours for the Prosperity of the British Empire he hopes may prove more successful.[243]

Lord North was convinced that abdication by the king because of a policy difference with Parliament, no matter how momentous the implications of that policy difference, would do great damage to the British constitution.[244] He wrote to the king:

The fate of the present Ministry is absolutely and irrevocably decided... your Majesty is well apprised that, in this country, the Prince on the Throne cannot, with prudence, oppose the deliberate resolution of the House of Commons.

The Parliament have altered their sentiments, and as their sentiments, whether just or erroneous, must ultimately prevail, Your Majesty having persevered, as long as possible, on what You thought right, can lose no honor if you yield at length, as some of the most renowned and glorious of your Predecessors have done, to the opinion and wishes of the House of Commons.[245]

Lord North, having defined the issue before the king as one of duty and patriotic responsibility, was able to persuade him to put away his letter of abdication and accept the rule of the House of Commons. The old ministry fell, and the opposition formed a new government that was committed to negotiate an end to the war and to end it on the basis of recognition of American independence. But of the various antiwar opposition blocs that might have taken power, the one most wary of compromise with the Americans formed the new government, under the leadership of the earl of Shelburne. Negotiations with the Americans, therefore, did not move along as smoothly or as quickly as they might have done otherwise. They got underway in Paris in the late spring of 1782 and were provisionally concluded in November that same year.

"HOW STRANGELY
ARE HUMAN AFFAIRS CONDUCTED"

While the negotiators in Europe discussed the terms for a settlement, the war in America went on. There were no major engagements, but there were many small-scale clashes, especially in the vicinity of the principal British garrisons, New York and Charleston, and in those clashes men fought and died. Among the Patriots who fell during this limbo period was Colonel John Laurens, who was killed in August 1782, at age twenty-seven, in a skirmish with a British foraging party on the Combahee River in South Carolina.

The leaders of the Revolution felt the loss of the courageous and idealistic Laurens with particular pain. He had joined General Washington's staff as an aide-de-camp in early August 1777 and was soon engaged in combat for the defense of Philadelphia, where he evinced a boldness that seemed to cross the line into recklessness. Lafayette witnessed Laurens's daring at the Battle at Brandywine and wrote about him, "It was not his fault that he was not killed or wounded[,] he did everything that was necessary to procure one or t'other."[246]

During the war, Laurens devised a plan to liberate the slaves through their enlistment in the Continental army. The concept had already proven itself in Rhode Island, and Laurens, a South Carolinian, proposed to extend the project to the large slave populations of the South. He wrote to his father in 1778 that his plan was "to augment the Continental Forces from [the slave population]…[in order to] advance those who are unjustly deprived of the Rights of Mankind [and]…reinforce the Defenders of Liberty with a number of gallant soldiers."

Laurens discussed this topic in some depth with General Washington, Alexander Hamilton and virtually anyone else who would listen, eventually bringing his proposal to the South Carolina legislature. How could the leaders of South Carolina, he asked, or of any state in the union, claim to be champions of liberty and yet be slave owners?

I think we Americans at least in the Southern Colonies, cannot contend with a good Grace, for Liberty, until we shall have enfranchised our Slaves. How can we whose Jealousy has been alarm'd more at the

Name of Oppression sometimes than at the Reality, reconcile to our spirited Assertions of the Rights of Mankind, the galling abject Slavery of our negroes.

When the South Carolina legislature rejected Laurens's proposal, he bitterly described their rejection as "the howlings of a triple-headed monster in which Prejudice, Avarice & Pusillanimity were united."[247]

Unfortunately for young Laurens and for the people of the United States, his plan for the abolition of slavery did not come to fruition in his lifetime. On learning of Laurens's death, Hamilton wrote to General Nathanael Greene: "I feel a deepest affliction at the news we have just received of the loss of our dear and [inesti]mable friend Laurens…his career of virtue is at an end. How strangely are human affairs conducted, that so many excellent qualities could not ensure a more happy fate?"[248]

THE SKIRMISH ON THE ICE

One of the last expeditions of Westchester militia and Westchester Guides occurred in mid-winter 1783, when some fifty Patriot horsemen made a bold effort to capture their nemesis, Loyalist leader Colonel James Delancey.[249] The winter had been severe; except for a channel of flowing water in the middle of the Hudson, the river was frozen solid.

The mounted militiamen and their commander, Captain Daniel Williams, followed the Guides through Westchester south to Delancey's house in West Farms (present-day Bronx). The operation was especially dangerous since it would not take place on "neutral ground" but well south of British lines. Among the Westchester Guides who pointed the way was the "Greenburgh Guide," John Odell, a man who was strikingly tall for that era, at "about six feet in height, and robust…capable of great and rapid exertion."[250]

Around midnight, the militiamen approached Delancey's house, but to no avail: the colonel was able to elude them. That's when their problems began, for the Patriot squad aroused Delancey's men. Pursued by the Delancey Loyalists, the Guides and militiamen sped north along the river road (Broadway), deep into Westchester County, trying to reach the Croton River and the relatively secure high country north of that river. But the Loyalists overtook the Patriot cavalry before they reached the Croton River and began to surround them.

Many decades later, in the 1840s and 1850s, the great Westchester chronicler John M. McDonald interviewed octogenarian eyewitnesses to the Hudson River clash that erupted that day. When Odell realized that he would soon be surrounded—so the interviewees told McDonald—he galloped onto the frozen Hudson, where he hoped to reach the shore above the Croton River. Two Loyalist horsemen sped onto the ice after him and tried to cut him off. Hotly pursued, Odell "rode toward the middle of the Hudson River, where the channel still remained unfrozen, determined, if the enemy persevered in the chase, to plunge into the water and make for the opposite shore," for he was not willing to become their captive.[251] One of Delancey's men caught up with Odell and swung his sword at him with awkward blows, which the Guide was able to ward off. Odell then "adopted the only expedient now left for escape, and drawing rein with all his might, threw his horse almost upon his haunches at the very moment when [the Loyalist] passed by. Arising in the stirrups, which were very short, the Guide of Greenberg now struck with his utmost force a blow at the royalist, which…cut through his cap and wounded him in the head. Stunned by the stroke, he reeled for a moment in the saddle and then fell upon the ice."[252] The other pursuer now swung his weapon at Odell, and again the Westchester Patriot was able to parry the blow. Remarkably, the Guide had stamina enough to speed away. He galloped north to safety, leaving Delancey's flummoxed men behind.

In the skirmish on the ice, the indomitable Odell had managed to save his life. In peacetime, he would purchase the house of the widow Bates, in present-day Hartsdale, Rochambeau's headquarters in July and August 1781. Known as the Odell House to this day, it preserves the memory of the widow, the general and the spirited Greenburgh Guide.

Fighting for the Mississippi

In their Paris negotiations with the representatives of the Shelburne ministry, the American commissioners—Benjamin Franklin, John Jay and John Adams—established several red lines and stood by them firmly.

One of the American red lines was not merely figurative but was an actual boundary line—the future western border of the United States. France and Spain were aware that the thirteen states wanted to make the Mississippi River their western border, and neither power liked the idea. Spain was especially averse to a Mississippi boundary for the united American states. Madrid claimed all of the territory to the west of the Mississippi and did not want to share the long river with an upstart confederation of thirteen aggressive republics on the eastern shore. Spain's foreign minister, the Conde de Floridablanca, confided that Spain would be willing to compromise: the boundary line could be west of the Alleghenies but certainly not as far west as the Mississippi. The French foreign minister, the Comte de Vergennes, supported Floridablanca on this point. Congress had instructed its Paris negotiators to seek the approval of the French court at all stages of the treaty negotiation. Adams and Jay considered this Congressional instruction to be outrageous, and they only pretended to accede to it, while actually ignoring it. (Franklin was at first troubled by his colleagues' circumvention of Congress and the French court but eventually, when he saw the positive results, joined Jay and Adams in the subterfuge.)

Fortunately for the United States, the decision regarding the western boundary would ultimately depend not on Spain or on France but only on Great Britain, since the trans-Allegheny territory was London's to keep or to yield. In the Paris negotiations, John Jay was the American commissioner who took the lead in advocating the Mississippi boundary. There might be room for compromise on other issues but not on this one, as far as he was concerned.

Shelburne's negotiators balked when Jay insisted on the Mississippi River border and suggested that the Americans accept, instead, a more easterly line. But Jay would have none of it: "If that line is insisted upon," he said, "it is needless to talk peace. We shall never accept it."[253] This was not a particularly diplomatic response, but it worked. The British commissioners went back to Shelburne, who consented to the Mississippi line. Much as Shelburne wished to preserve, insofar as possible, British assets in North America, he most of all desired to bring the negotiations to a conclusion, present a peace treaty to Parliament for its approval and ratification and end the war.

Left: Portrait of John Jay by Gilbert Stuart, 1794. Jay was forty-nine years old in 1794 and was serving as the first chief justice of the United States. *Wikimedia Commons*.

Below: Boundaries of the United States as determined by the Treaty of Paris (ratified, 1783). Copyright 2011 by Richard Borkow.

Claimed by Russia, Great Britain and Spain

British America

Spanish Territories

United States

Because of the victory at Yorktown, which had laid the groundwork, and because of John Jay's firmness in Paris, the trans-Allegheny territories were secured for the United States, and the threat of *uti possidetis* was finally and categorically eradicated.

"IT WILL NOT BE BELIEVED"

With the war about to end, Washington pondered the eight terrible years of conflict and wondered how so ragged a force as the Continental army could have triumphed in the end. Writing to General Greene in January 1783, he speculated that posterity would find the historical facts hard to believe:

> *If historiographers should be hardy enough to fill the pages of History with the advantages that have been gained with unequal numbers (on the part of America) in the course of this contest, and attempt to relate the distressing circumstances under which they have been obtained, it is more than probable that Posterity will bestow on their labors the epithet and marks of fiction; for it will not be believed, that such a force as Great Britain has employed for eight years in this Country could be baffled in their plan of subjugating it, by numbers infinitely less, composed of Men oftentimes half starved, always in Rags, without pay, and experiencing every species of distress, which human nature is capable of undergoing.*[254]

NOTES

ACKNOWLEDGEMENTS

1. www.youtube.com/watch?v=GxX0Kzfyeyk&feature=related.

INTRODUCTION

2. A sloop is a sailboat with a single mast located toward the front of the boat.
3. Diamant, *Chaining the Hudson*, 21.
4. Abbatt, *Memoirs of Major General William Heath*, 60, 61.
5. Diamant, *Chaining the Hudson*, 33.
6. Ibid., 35.
7. French, *History of Westchester County*, 119. (quoting Ralph Burrell.)
8. British regional dominance in 1777 ended abruptly in December when the British high command, staggered by the defeat at Saratoga, abandoned the captured forts and pulled back to Manhattan.
9. Scharf, *History of Westchester County*.
10. University of Michigan, William L. Clements Library, Sir Henry Clinton Papers, Volume 26, item 40. www.royalprovincial.com/military/rhist/emmerick/emmlet2.htm.
11. Swanson, *Between the Lines*, 33.
12. freepages.genealogy.rootsweb.ancestry.com/~vantasselfamilyhistory homepage/Revolution.html.

13. Jewell, *The Sawmill River Valley War*, 102.
14. Thacher, *Military Journal*, November 24–27, 1780, 237.
15. Ibid., 256.
16. The Sprain Brook Parkway passes through the gorge today.
17. Closen, *Revolutionary Journal*.
18. The campaign of 1781 would almost certainly be the last unless the Americans decided to go it alone—this option had become almost inconceivable by 1781.
19. Ferling, *Almost a Miracle*, 472.
20. Kruger, "New York Slavery."

CHAPTER 1

21. Clary, *Adopted Son*, 75.
22. Stainville was French foreign minister until 1770. Vergennes became foreign minister in 1774.
23. Unger, *Lafayette*, 17.
24. Montross, *Reluctant Rebels*, 119.
25. Ibid., 144.
26. The triumph may have been unambiguous in Massachusetts. But every phase of the war, including the first, saw a mixture of victory and disaster. While Boston was under siege, an American army was soundly repulsed at the walls of Québec in December 1775. And six months earlier, at the Battle of Bunker Hill, the Americans, after driving back three British assaults, had to retreat from the battleground. British losses were so ghastly that the Battle of Bunker Hill amounted to a strategic defeat for the British.
27. McCullough, *1776*, 142, 143.
28. London sent the Howe brothers to America with an odd double mission: they were to be its conquerors, but at the same time, they were empowered to discuss peace terms with the rebels. The double mission did not work out very well. The fact that the Howes' peace terms consisted of nothing more than an offer to pardon the rebels (except, of course, for a few really bad ones) didn't help to convince Congress.
29. McCullough, *1776*, 191.
30. *New England Chronicle*, September 19, 1776: "Providence favored us." Quoted in McCullough, *1776*, 196.
31. The third attempt was thwarted at Pell's Point by the brave and effective defense offered by a small band of Massachusetts men under the command of Colonel John Glover.

32. Excerpt from letter to the president of the Continental Congress, September 1778.
33. Clary, *Adopted Son*, 83. Lafayette had too much respect for royal authority to defy a warrant issued by the king. Rather, he allowed himself to be convinced that no warrant had actually been issued.
34. Ibid., 81.
35. Arthur Lee was a third Congressional emissary in Paris, but he displayed frankly paranoid tendencies and was more disruptive than helpful.
36. Quoted in Bobrick, *Angel in the Whirlwind*, 295.
37. Unger, *Lafayette*, 45, 46.
38. Through his marriage to the widow Martha Custis, Washington did have a stepdaughter and a stepson.

Chapter 2

39. The principal American defeats in 1777 were at Ticonderoga on Lake Champlain; at Fort Montgomery on the Hudson; at Fort Mifflin, located on an island in the Delaware River; at Brandywine, south of Philadelphia, at Paoli; and at Germantown. Following the defeat at Brandywine, General Howe was able to enter the American capital, Philadelphia, unopposed, and his army occupied the city. The Continental Congress was forced to flee, first to Lancaster, Pennsylvania, and then to York, Pennsylvania.
40. Schiff, *Great Improvisation*, 5. A large arms shipment from France, bound for Saratoga, was carried by a vessel, which broke though the British blockade and unloaded its weapons and ammunition at Portsmouth, New Hampshire.
41. Jackson and Twohig, eds., *George Washington Papers at the Library of Congress*, John Adams to George Washington, January 6, 1776.
42. Willcox, *American Rebellion*, 12.
43. Ibid., 11.
44. The American minister George Germain bears at least partial responsibility for the plan's failure, for he did not issue clear orders to General Howe. Whether Germain or Howe was more at fault for the British disaster at Saratoga is a question that has been debated for more than two centuries. Burgoyne has not escaped criticism because of his tactical mistakes and because of his dismissive view of American capabilities. The British commander in Canada, General Guy Carleton, has also been blamed because he stinted in his support

for Burgoyne. Even George Bernard Shaw has contributed to the debate. In his play *The Devil's Disciple*, Shaw assigned virtually all of the blame to Germain.

45. Lossing, *Empire State*, 281. 2,400 of the surrendering troops were Germans.

46. www.americanheritage.com/articles/magazine/ah/1964/2/1964_2 _6.shtml. "N. Army" here refers to Burgoyne's army.

47. The thirteen colonies were rich jewels in the crown of the Empire. But they were not the richest. The West Indian sugar islands generated more wealth for Great Britain than did the thirteen colonies.

48. Montross, *Reluctant Rebels*, 235.

49. Marching across New Jersey from Philadelphia, the British were attacked by General Washington's army at the Battle of Monmouth.

50. Ships of the line were the great sailing battleships of the era, and they reflected national power upon the seas. A vessel was worthy of the term "ship of the line" only if it was sufficiently armed to take a position in the line of battle. In the early decades of the eighteenth century, ships of the line might contain as few as 50 guns, but by the latter decades of the century 60 guns were viewed as the minimum requirement. The largest ships of the line carried as many as 120 guns. The guns were arranged on several decks. The ships that had 80 or more guns would typically have three decks. Coggins, *Ships and Seamen of the American Revolution*.

51. The Jacob Purdy House is preserved today in a serene setting on Park Avenue in White Plains.

52. Baker, *Itinerary of General Washington*, 140.

53. Bonsal, *When the French Were Here*, 45.

54. Dull, *Diplomatic History of the American Revolution*, 110.

55. Ibid., 109.

56. Ibid., 113.

57. An initial attempt to seize Canada by American generals Montgomery and Arnold failed in December 1775.

58. In Weintraub, *Iron Tears*, 170; in Tuchman, *March of Folly*, 224.

59. British leaders regularly referred to General Washington as "Mr. Washington," loath to disguise their contempt for the rebellion and its commander.

60. Willcox, *American Rebellion*, 87.

61. Moran, "Storming of Stony Point," www.revolutionarywararchives. org/stonypoint.html.

62. Colonel Johnston was the British commander at Stony Point.

63. Moran, "Storming of Stony Point."
64. Willcox, *American Rebellion*, 133.
65. Lancaster, *From Lexington to Liberty*, 384.
66. Baker, *Itinerary of General Washington*, 177. James Duane was a delegate to the Continental Congress representing New York. He is memorably portrayed in the *John Adams* HBO video series (based on David McCullough's *John Adams*) when the vote was taken to approve American independence. On that occasion, Duane stated that New York "respectfully abstains."
67. Admiral Ternay died at Newport in December 1780 of a febrile illness, and the command of the French warships in Rhode Island passed to the ranking captain of the fleet, M. Destouches. Several months later, in May 1781, Destouches turned over command to Admiral Barras, who had arrived in Newport that month from France.

CHAPTER 3

68. A *coup de main* is a sudden attack in force.
69. Rose, *Washington's Spies*, 190.
70. Lancaster, *American Revolution*, 313.
71. Bonsal, *When the French Were Here*, 27.
72. Ibid., 27, 28.
73. Irving, *Life of George Washington*, vol. 4, 106.
74. The depreciation of the American currency was due, in part, to a large-scale counterfeiting effort on the part of the British in New York, which was brought to Washington's attention by the Culper Ring.
75. Rose, *Washington's Spies*, 182.
76. Ibid., 184.
77. Bonsal, *When the French Were Here*, 34.
78. Ibid., 19. Messages to and from France were sent through the port of Boston.
79. Bonsal, *When the French Were Here*, 31.
80. Bernier, *Lafayette, Hero of Two Worlds*, 101.
81. Bonsal, *When the French Were Here*, 31.
82. Rose, *Washington's Spies*, 196.
83. Flexner, *Traitor and the Spy*, 333.
84. At times of American dominance in the region, Washington preferred to establish his southernmost Hudson post at Dobbs Ferry in order to facilitate communication and transport across the river. The Americans had been ascendant in the region ever since full

implementation of the southern strategy, which began in late 1779, and led to concentration of British troops in the southern states and relative quiescence in the North.

85. Peggy's role as Arnold's dedicated co-conspirator did not come to light until the 1920s, when scholars read Sir Henry Clinton's war documents, purchased in 1923 by William Clements for the University of Michigan library. Why was Peggy not suspected? One reason was her magnificent thespian skills. On the day he learned of Arnold's betrayal, Washington and his entourage arrived at the Arnold home expecting to confer with him over breakfast. Only Peggy was at home. The Arnolds had just found out that the treason had been exposed, and appreciating the danger of imminent arrest, Arnold was fleeing to New York. It was only later that day that an astonished Washington saw Andre's papers. "Arnold has betrayed us!" he cried out in shock. "Whom can we trust now?" Peggy now gave the best acting performance of the war, playing the role of a distraught wife, driven mad and delusional on hearing the news of her husband's treachery. In bed, disheveled and in a state of near undress, she raved and wept, pleading for Washington's help: a "hot iron" had been put on her head, she said, and only he could remove it. When the commander in chief went upstairs to calm her, she became frantic, crying out that Washington had come to kill her infant son and that her husband had gone "up there" (the ceiling) and would never return. For Hamilton, Mrs. Arnold's unhinged behavior "was the most affecting scene I ever was witness to" and "would have pierced insensibility itself." She was given safe passage to her father's home in Philadelphia and soon was able to join her husband in New York. Chernow, *Washington: A Life*, 381.

86. Shonnard and Spooner, *History of Westchester County*, 480.

87. Ibid., 333.

88. Light Horse Harry Lee was twenty-four years old in October 1780. In 1807, at age fifty-one, he would become the father of Robert E. Lee.

89. Hallahan, *Day the Revolution Ended*, 25.

90. Eventually, Champe was able to escape from the British camp and get himself to American lines.

91. Fitzpatrick, ed., *Writings of George Washington from the Original Manuscript Sources*. Camp at Cambridge, July 10, 1775.

92. Augur, *The Secret War of Independence*, New York: Duell, Sloan and Pearce, 1955, 36.

93. McDougall, *Freedom Just around the Corner*, 257.

CHAPTER 4

94. Westchester County then included all of its present territory, plus all of the Bronx.
95. Shonnard and Spooner, *History of Westchester County*, 297.
96. The Stamp Act Congress of 1765, which had successfully dealt with a similar crisis, served as an encouraging precedent.
97. Hufeland, *Westchester County*, 13.
98. Ibid.
99. Columbia University today.
100. www.upa.pdx.edu/IMS/currentprojects/TAHv3/TAH_Course/20 10_Materials/Seabury_Letter_Jan_1775.pdf.
101. Quoted in Chernow, *Alexander Hamilton*.
102. The Patriots tried to block passage of warships up the Hudson by placing obstacles at Fort Washington and by constructing two chain barriers: one just north of Peekskill and the other near West Point. The chain at West Point was never tested, but the other barriers proved ineffective.
103. News from Rhode Island of the Sullivan-d'Estaing fracas had boosted British spirits. The shattering impact of the defeat at Saratoga was wearing off. D'Estaing's fleet, which was presumed at first to be a great threat, seemed incapable of doing any damage to the Crown.
104. Hufeland, *Westchester County*, 259.
105. Ibid., 260.
106. Baker, *Itinerary of General Washington*, 140.
107. Hufeland, *Westchester County*, 266.
108. Willcox, *American Rebellion*, xxxi. Clinton's capture of Stony Point and Fort Lafayette in May 1779 was the prelude for the intense British attacks in the region during the summer of 1779 (see page 54).
109. Hufeland, *Westchester County*, 294.
110. Ibid., 295.
111. Shonnard and Spooner, *History of Westchester County*, 458.
112. Enoch Crosby appears to have been the model for James Fenimore Cooper's Harvey Birch, the resourceful protagonist of his 1821 novel, *The Spy*.
113. Barnum, *The Spy Unmasked*, 56.
114. In 1926, Tarrytown historian William Abbatt published a monograph on the strike at Four Corners and described the attacking regular troops as "the flower of the British army—the light infantry and the grenadiers." Abbatt, *Attack on Youngs' House (or Four Corners)*.

115. A similarly devastating loss, also due to a Delancey raid, was suffered at Pine's Bridge on the Croton in May 1781.
116. Ibid.

CHAPTER 5

117. Sparks, *Writings of George Washington*, 120. books.google.com/books?id=7L7syZvM0PwC&printsec=frontcover&dq=inauthor:%22Jared+Sparks%22&hl=en&ei=SMYdTcZiw4CUB_CXycEL&sa=X&oi=book_result&ct=result&resnum=1&ved=0CC4Q6AEwAA#v=onepage&q&f=false.
118. Bonsal, *When the French Were Here*, 32.
119. The July 8 letter was written from the Lower Westchester Encampment.
120. Fitzpatrick, *Writings of George Washington*, 340.
121. Marshall, *Life of George Washington*, 376. www.gutenberg.org/files/18593/18593-h/18593-h.htm.
122. Klos, "President Who? Forgotten Founders." www.virtualology.com/declarationofindependence/SamuelHuntington.org.
123. General Anthony Wayne, commander of the Pennsylvania line, wrote to Washington at 4:30 a.m. on January 2, 1781, that most of the Pennsylvania troops had mutinied. There were altogether about 2,500 troops in the line; Montross states that 1,300 mutinied. See Flexner, *George Washington in the American Revolution*, 405, 406; Freeman, *George Washington*, 236, 249; and Montross, *Story of the Continental Army*, 394.
124. Freeman, *George Washington*, 237.
125. Stone, *Our French Allies*, 357.
126. Flexner, *George Washington in the American Revolution*, 407.
127. Freeman, *George Washington*, 243.
128. Ibid., 245.
129. Ibid.; Flexner, *George Washington in the American Revolution*, 408.
130. Thacher, *Military Journal*.
131. Ibid.
132. Ibid.
133. Montross, *Reluctant Rebels*, 293.
134. Adams, *Works of John Adams*, vol. 7, 429.
135. John Adams, April 15, 1809, in letter to editor of the *Literary World*.
136. Montross, *Reluctant Rebels*, 320.
137. Ferling writes that if the principle of *uti possidetis* had been applied in the spring of 1781, it was likely that Great Britain would have retained

control of New York City and Long Island, the trans-Appalachian west, the Penobscot region (of present-day Maine), northern New York state, northern Vermont, Georgia and the Carolinas. Ferling, *Almost a Miracle*, 472, 473.

138. Ibid.

139. Flexner, *George Washington in the American Revolution*, 423; letter from George Washington to Thomas Jefferson concerning the risk to Virginia from implementation of the principle of *uti possidetis*: memory. loc.gov/cgi-bin/query/r?ammem/mgw:@field%28DOCID+@ lit%28gw220210%29%29.

140. Destouches became naval chief after the death of Admiral Ternay in December 1780.

141. In early March 1781, Washington traveled to Newport to meet a second time with General Rochambeau. The American commander made the trip because he hoped that his presence in Newport would give a gentle nudge to the French and speed the departure of the eight warships to the Chesapeake. He was in Newport when the ships left on March 8.

142. Flexner, *Washington*, 152.

143. Ibid.

144. Fitzpatrick, *Writings of George Washington*. George Washington to John Laurens, New Windsor, April 9, 1781. The Washington Papers, Library of Congress.

145. Fox was adapting the phrasing from the Roman historian Plutarch.

146. Cook, *The Long Fuse*, 333.

147. Ibid., 335.

148. Ibid.

149. Stanhope, *History of England*, 115, quoting Sir Henry Clinton's memoirs.

150. Rochambeau's son was the Vicomte de Rochambeau.

151. Freeman, *George Washington*, 286.

152. General Washington at Tappan to General Heath, August 8, 1780. Baker, *Itinerary of General Washington*, 185.

153. Artificers are craftsmen or workmen.

154. General Washington at Tappan to General Arnold, August 11, 1780. Baker, *Itinerary of General Washington*, 186.

155. Freeman, *George Washington*, 285 and 286.

CHAPTER 6

156. Wethersfield, Connecticut, is about five miles south of Hartford.

157. Freeman, *George Washington*, 288.

158. Quoted in Bonsal, *When the French Were Here*, 83. The generals communicated by writing lists of questions to each other and then preparing written responses, assisted by their bilingual aides.
159. British general William Phillips, who had joined Arnold a couple of months earlier and who had been participating with him in the pillaging of Virginia, died of typhus on May 15 at Petersburg, a few days before Cornwallis arrived.
160. Freeman, *George Washington*, 292, note 57.
161. Flexner, *George Washington in the American Revolution*, 428.
162. Ibid., 433.
163. Ibid., 428.
164. Quoted in Miller, *U.S. Navy*, 13
165. Davis, *The Campaign that Won America*, 16.
166. Flexner, *George Washington in the American Revolution*, 432.
167. Quoted in Lewis, *Admiral De Grasse*, 131.
168. Quoted in Davis, *The Campaign that Won America*, 17.
169. Fitzpatrick, *Diaries of George Washington*, 217.
170. Cook, *The Long Fuse*, 338.
171. Freeman, *George Washington*, 291.
172. Cook, *The Long Fuse*, 338.
173. Ensign John Moody
174. Thacher, *Military Journal*, 256.
175. Freeman, *George Washington*, 292, note 56.
176. Quoted in Davis, *Campaign that Won America*, 36.
177. In earlier correspondence, Clinton expressed a preference for Yorktown as the location of the naval base.
178. Quoted in Fleming, *Beat the Last Drum*, 57.
179. Willcox, *American Rebellion*, 536.
180. Ibid., 541.
181. The letters from Lafayette revealing that Cornwallis was successively in Williamsburg, Jamestown, Portsmouth and finally Yorktown were received on July 9, July 23, August 6 and August 16, respectively.

CHAPTER 7

182. There were two regiments in each brigade. The Boubonnais and the Royal Deux-Ponts regiments composed the First Brigade,
183. The Soissonais and Saintonge regiments comprised the Second Brigade.
184. The Legion of Lauzun did not depart from Newport but from Lebanon, Connecticut, where it had been based since November

1780. Along the line of march it kept ten to fifteen miles south of the main army.

185. Closen, *Revolutionary Journal*, xxiv; Davis, *The Campaign that Won America*, 6.

186. Closen, *Revolutionary Journal*, 87.

187. Thacher, *Military Journal*, 265.

188. Closen, *Revolutionary Journal*, 90.

189. Bonsal, *When the French Were Here*, 110.

190. Donovan, *George Washington at "Head Quarters, Dobbs Ferry,"* 21. "Left" meant east, since the two armies faced the British to the south.

191. Ibid., 21.

192. George Washington Papers at the Library of Congress. memory. loc.gov/cgi-bin/query/r?ammem/mgw:@field%28DOCID+@ lit%28gw220350%29%29.

193. Rice and Brown, *American Campaigns*, vol. I, 32.

194. Closen, *Revolutionary Journal*, 90.

195. Ibid., 91.

196. Not to be confused with modern-day Dobbs Ferry Road, which follows an east–west course a mile or so to the north of Heatherdell Road.

197. Massachusetts Historical Society, Adams electronic archive. www.masshist.org/digitaladams/aea/cfm/doc.cfm?id=D22B&numr ecs=1&archive=all&hi=on&mode=&query=dobbs%20ferry&queryi d=&rec=1&start=1&tag=text#firstmatch.

198. Casey, Thomas F.X, "A Brief History of Rockland County." www. familyhistory101.com/county/ny-county-rockland.html.

199. Selig, *Washington-Rochambeau Revolutionary Route*, 91. "Of the Appleby house there are only stone fences and cellar holes left from the farm on the wooded lot behind the WFAS radio station."

200. Johnson and Brown, *The Twentieth Century Biographical Dictionary of Notable Americans*, vol. 8, identifies Jonathan Odell as John Odell's father. www.VillageHistorian.org shows 1779 boundaries of Jonathan Odell's homestead. (See Historic Maps section.)

The Westchester Guides were native sons of Westchester County familiar with its roads and terrain who served as "military conductors," guiding American forces, and later French forces as well, along the best routes for military operations. The earliest documented American movement in the county that was assisted by the Guides was General William Heath's attempt against the British fortifications near Kingsbridge in January 1777. John Odell of Irvington was one of the leading Guides for that operation and continued to serve in the capacity of a Guide throughout the war. In July 1781, he directed the American contingent of the Grand Reconnaissance. (See later section of this chapter. For his activities in 1783 and after, see epilogue. John Odell was also known as the "Greenburgh Guide.") Hadaway, *McDonald Papers*, 66–97. The Harmse-Odell House still stands at the corner of Broadway and Dows Lane in Irvington. Spikes and Leone, *Irvington*, 11.

201. Selig, *Washington-Rochambeau Revolutionary Route*, 91. Dr. Selig writes that most of the French troops were encamped on the Tompkins farm, referring to the property of John Tompkins, which lay immediately to the southeast of the property of the widow Bates. The adjacent Tompkins and Bates properties are shown on a 1779 map of the area, which can be found on the VillageHistorian.org website. The map was provided courtesy of Westchester County Archives: www.villagehistorian.org/ Historic%20Maps/Map%20of%20Dobbs%20Ferry%201779%20 %28Manor%20of%20Philipsborough%290001.pdf.

202. Rice, and Brown, *American Campaigns of Rochambeau's Armies*. Plate 41 shows the "Legion de Sheldon" on summit of Villard Hill.

203. Ibid., 249. Louis-Alexandre Berthier would go on to great fame. In 1796, Napoleon made Berthier his chief of staff. And in 1804, when Napoleon became emperor, he immediately named Berthier marshal of France.

204. Moore, *Diary of the American Revolution*, 459.

205. Ibid.

206. Ibid., 460.

207. Thacher, *Military Journal*, 267.

208. Gouverneur Morris, a major figure at the Constitutional Convention of 1787, would draft the preamble to the Constitution of the United States.

209. Rice and Brown, *American Campaigns of Rochambeau's Armies*, 253.

210. Fitzpatrick, *Diaries of George Washington*, 239.

211. "North River" was Washington's usual term for the Hudson River.

212. Fort Knyphausen was previously called Fort Washington. Today it is the location of the eastern ramps of the George Washington Bridge.

CHAPTER 8

213. Bobrick, *Angel in the Whirlwind*, 448.

214. Fitzpatrick, *Diaries of George Washington*, 248.

215. Ibid., 249.

216. Ibid.

217. Ibid., 241.

218. Ephraim Blain, commissary general for the army, and James Wilson, legal advocate for French forces in America, were part of the entourage that accompanied Morris and Peters to the Westchester camps.

219. Simpson, *Lives of Eminent Philadelphians*, 706.

220. Hallahan, *Day the Revolution Ended*, 143.

221. Jackson and Twohig, George Washington Papers. Vol. III.

222. Quoted in Upham, *Life of General Washington*, 35.

223. Selig, *Washington-Rochambeau Revolutionary Route*, 148. Selig concurs that the troops coming out of Ardsley on August 19 marched along Ashford Avenue toward the Ashford Avenue–Broadway intersection and were given the puzzling orders to turn to the right and north at that intersection. Baron von Closen's *Revolutionary Journal*, 107, states that Washington's army "left the Philipsburg camp…marching by the Tarrytown road, along the river." The road north from Dobbs Ferry to Tarrytown is today's Broadway. Davis, *Campaign that Won America*, 74.

224. Selig, *Washington, Rochambeau, and the Yorktown Campaign*, 1, 24. Scammel's light infantry, Olney's Rhode Island regiment, Hazen's Canadian regiment, Lamb's artillery, Van Schaik's first New York regiment and Ogden's combined New Jersey regiment were among the American army units that were paraded for the march and left for Virginia from Dobbs Ferry on August 19, 1781.

225. Thacher, *Military Journal*, 269. In this video interview on YouTube, David Hackett Fischer discusses the meaning of "parade for the march," as the term was understood during the Revolutionary War: www.youtube.com/watch?v=GxX0Kzfyeyk.

226. Bobrick, *Angel in the Whirlwind*, 448.

227. Eckenrode, *Story of the Campaign and Siege of Yorktown*.

228. Davis, *Campaign that Won America*, 24.

229. Ibid., 26.

230. Ibid., 28.

231. Chidsey, *Victory at Yorktown*, 117.

232. Davis, *Campaign that Won America*, 30.

233. Rappleye, *Robert Morris*, 260. News of the arrival in the Chesapeake Bay of de Grasse, who was conveying specie borrowed in Havana, also improved American credit, and Rochambeau lent funds to the American army from his war chest.

234. While de Grasse had brought twenty-eight ships of the line into the Chesapeake, only twenty-four of them were in the vicinity of the Capes on September 5 when Graves arrived.

235. Lafayette's troops, Anthony Wayne's reconstituted Pennsylvania line, the 3,500 French troops from the West Indies and Virginia state militia pouring into the area totaled about 7,000 men.

236. Quoted in Davis, *Campaign that Won America*, 197.

237. Ibid.,

238. Rice and Brown, *American Campaigns of Rochambeau's Army*, 6.

239. Lumpkin, *From Savannah to Yorktown*, 307. At the urging of Washington and Rochambeau, de Grasse ultimately consented to remain in the Chesapeake Bay until November 1. (see text, page 143)

EPILOGUE

240. Cook, *The Long Fuse*, 384.

241. Irving, *Life of George Washington*, 621. Irving is reporting George Germain's account of Lord North's reaction.

242. Fleming, *Perils of Peace*, 136.

243. Cook, *The Long Fuse*, 355.

244. The British constitution is not a single document but the many documents of law and precedent that determine how Great Britain is governed.

245. Cook, *The Long Fuse*, 356.

246. Massey, *John Laurens and the American Revolution*, 75.

247. Ibid., 208.

248. Ibid., 230.

249. Hadaway, *The McDonald Papers*, 82.

250. Ibid., 84. (John Odell's activities earlier in the war are described in Chapter 7.)

251. Ibid., 83.

252. Ibid., 84.

253. Cook, *The Long Fuse*, 370.

254. Quoted in Ellis, *His Excellency*, 111.

BIBLIOGRAPHY

Abbatt, William. *The Attack on Youngs' House (or Four Corners) February 3, 1780; An Episode of the Neutral Ground.* Tarrytown, PA: W. Abbatt, 1926.
———, ed. *Memoirs of Major General William Heath.* New York: Abbatt, 1901.
Adams, Charles Francis. *The Works of John Adams, Second President of the United States.* Vol. 7. Boston: Little, Brown & Co., 1852.
Augur, Helen. *The Secret War of Independence.* New York: Duell, Sloan and Pearce, 1955
Baker, William S. *Itinerary of General Washington from June 15, 1775, to December 23, 1783.* Copyright, 1892. Reprinted, Lambertville, NJ: Hunterdon House, 1970.
Barnum, H.L. *The Spy Unmasked.* Harrison, NY: Harbor Hill Books, 1975.
Bernier, Olivier. *Lafayette, Hero of Two Worlds.* New York: E.P. Dutton, 1983.
Bobrick, Benson. *Angel in the Whirlwind.* New York: Simon and Schuster, 1997.
Bonsal, Stephen. *When the French Were Here.* Garden City, NY: Doubleday Doran & Co., 1945.
Chastellux, François-Jean. *Travels in North America, Volume 1, American Revolutionary War Series.* Bedford MA: Applewood, 1828.
———. *Travels in North America in the Years 1780, 1781 and 1782.* Chapel Hill: University of North Carolina Press, 1963.
Chernow, Ron. *Alexander Hamilton.* New York: Penguin Books, 2004.

Chidsey, Donald Barr. *Victory at Yorktown*. New York: Crown Publishers, 1962.

Clary, David A. *Adopted Son: Washington, Lafayette and the Friendship That Saved the Revolution*. New York: Bantam Books, 2007.

Closen, Baron Ludwig von. *The Revolutionary Journal of Baron Ludwig von Closen, 1780–1783*. Edited and translated by Evelyn M. Acomb. Chapel Hill: University of North Carolina Press, 1958.

Coggins, Jack. *Ships and Seamen of the American Revolution*. Harrisburg, PA: Stackpole Books, 1969.

Cook, Don. *The Long Fuse: How England Lost the American Colonies, 1760–1785*. New York: Atlantic Monthly Press, 1995.

Cresson, W.P. *Francis Dana: A Puritan Diplomat at the Court of Catherine the Great*. New York: Dial Press, 1930.

Dann, John C., ed. *The Revolution Remembered; Eyewitness Accounts of the War for Independence*. Chicago: University of Chicago Press, 1977.

Davis, Burke. *The Campaign that Won America*. New York: Dial Press, 1970.

Diamant, Lincoln. *Chaining the Hudson: The Fight for the River in the American Revolution*. New York: Carol Publishing Group, 1989.

Donovan, Mary Sudman. *George Washington at "Head Quarters, Dobbs Ferry."* Bloomington, IN: iUniverse, 2009.

Dull, Jonathan R. *A Diplomatic History of the American Revolution*. New Haven, CT: Yale University Press, 1985.

Dupuy, R. Ernest, and Trevor N. Dupuy. *The Compact History of the Revolutionary War*. New York: Hawthorn Books, Inc., 1963.

Eckenrode, H.J. *The Story of the Campaign and Siege of Yorktown*. Washington, D.C.: United States Senate, Senate document No. 318, 1931.

Ellis, Joseph J. *His Excellency: George Washington*. New York: Random House, 2004.

Ferling, John. *Almost a Miracle*. New York: Oxford University Press, 2007.
———. *Setting the World Ablaze*. New York: Oxford University Press, 2000.

Fischer, David Hackett. *Albion's Seed: Four British Folkways in America*. New York: Oxford University Press, 1989.
———. *Paul Revere's Ride*. New York: Oxford University Press, 1994.
———. *Washington's Crossing*. New York: Oxford University Press, 2004.

Fitzpatrick, John C., ed. *The Diaries of George Washington 1748–1799*. Boston: Houghton-Mifflin Company, 1925.
———. *The Writings of George Washington from the Original Manuscripts, 1745–1799*. Vol. 22. Washington, D.C.: Library of Congress, 1937.

Fleming, Thomas J. *Beat the Last Drum: The Siege of Yorktown in 1781*. New York: St. Martin's Press, 1963.

———. *The Perils of Peace, America's Struggle for Survival after Yorktown*. New York: HarperCollins, 2007.

Flexner, James Thomas. *George Washington in the American Revolution, 1775–1783*. Boston: Little, Brown and Company, 1968.

———. *The Traitor and the Spy*. Boston: Little, Brown and Company, 1952.

———. *Washington: The Indispensable Man*. Boston: Little, Brown and Company, 1974.

Freeman, Douglas Southall. *George Washington: A Biography*. Vol. 5. New York, 1952.

French, Alvah P., ed. *History of Westchester County, New York*. New York: Lewis Historical Publishing Company, 1925.

Hadaway, William S., ed. *The McDonald Papers, Part One*. White Plains, NY: Westchester County Historical Society, 1926.

Hallahan, William H. *The Day the Revolution Ended*. Hoboken, NJ: John Wiley and Sons, 2004.

Hibbert, Christopher. *Redcoats and Rebels: The American Revolution through British Eyes*. New York: W.W. Norton & Co., 1990.

Hufeland, Otto. *Westchester County during the American Revolution*. Harrison, NY: Harbor Hills Books, 1982.

Irving, Washington. *Life of George Washington*. New York: G.P. Putnam's Sons, 1859.

Jackson, Donald, and Dorothy Twohig, eds. *George Washington Papers at the Library of Congress, 1741–1799: The Diaries of George Washington*. Vol. III. 1771–75; 1780–81. Charlottesville: University Press of Virginia, 1978.

Jewell, Roger L. *The Sawmill River Valley War*. Fairfield, PA: Jewell Histories, 2009.

Johnson, Rossiter, and John H. Brown, eds. *The Twentieth Century Biographical Dictionary of Notable Americans*. Vol. 8. Boston: Biographical Society, 1904.

Ketchum, Richard M. *Victory at Yorktown: The Campaign That Won the Revolution*. New York: Henry Holt & Co., 2004.

Klos, Stanley L. "President Who? Forgotten Founders." www.virtualology.com/declarationofindependence/SamuelHuntington.org.

Knollenberg, Bernhard. *Washington and the Revolution*. New York: Macmillan Company, 1940.

Kruger, Vivienne L. "New York Slavery." PhD thesis, Columbia University, 2007. newyorkslavery.blogspot.com/2007/08/chapter-four.html.

Lancaster, Bruce. *The American Revolution*. Boston: Houghton, Mifflin, 2001.

————. *From Lexington to Liberty*. Garden City, NY: Doubleday & Co., 1955.

Leckie, Robert. *George Washington's War: The Saga of the American Revolution*. New York: HarperCollins, 1993.

Lecky, William Edward Hartpole. *The American Revolution, 1763/1783*. Edited by James Woodburn. New York: D. Appleton & Co., 1898.

Lewis, Charles Lee. *Admiral De Grasse and American Independence*. Manchester NH: Ayer Publishing, 1980.

Lossing, Benson. *The Empire State: A Compendious History of the Commonwealth of New York*. Hartford, CT: American Publishing Company, 1888.

Lumpkin, Henry. *From Savannah to Yorktown: The American Revolution in the South*. Columbia: University of South Carolina Press, 1981.

Marshall, John. *The Life of George Washington*. Vol. 3. 1805–1807. Reprint, Fredericksburg, VA: Citizens' Guild of Washington's Boyhood Home, 1926. www.gutenberg.org/files/18593/18593-h/18593-h.htm.

Massey, Gregory D. *John Laurens and the American Revolution*. Columbia: University of South Carolina Press, 2000.

McCullough, David. *1776*. New York: Simon and Schuster, 2005.

McDougall, Walter A. *Freedom Just around the Corner: A New American History, 1585–1828*. New York: HarperCollins, 2004.

Meltzer, Milton, ed. *The American Revolutionaries: A History in Their Own Words 1750–1800*. New York: HarperCollins, 1987

Miller, Nathan. *The U.S. Navy: A History*. Annapolis, MD: Naval Institute Press, 1997.

Montross, Lynn. *The Reluctant Rebels*. New York: Harper and Brothers, 1950.

————. *The Story of the Continental Army 1775–1783*. New York: Barnes & Noble, 1952.

Moore, Frank. *Diary of the American Revolution: From News Papers and Original Documents*. New York: Charles T. Evans, 1863.

Moran, Donald N. "The Storming of Stony Point." www.revolutionarywararchives.org/stonypoint.html.

Rappleye, Charles. *Robert Morris*. New York: Simon & Schuster, 2010.

Rice, Howard C., Jr., and Anne S.K. Brown, eds. and trans. *The American Campaigns of Rochambeau's Army*. Vols. 1 and 2. Princeton, NJ: Princeton University Press, 1972.

Rose, Alexander. *Washington's Spies: The Story of America's First Spy Ring*. New York: Bantam Dell, 2006.

Scharf, John Thomas. *History of Westchester County*. Philadelphia: L.E. Preston and Co., 1886.

Schechter, Stephen L., ed. *Roots of the Republic: American Founding Documents Interpreted*. Madison, WI: Madison House Publishers, 1990.

Schecter, Barnet. *The Battle for New York: The City at the Heart of the American Revolution*. New York: Penguin Books, 2003.

Schiff, Stacy. *A Great Improvisation: Franklin, France, and the Birth of America*. New York: Henry Holt & Co., 2005.

Selby, John. *The Road to Yorktown*. New York: St. Martin's Press, 1776.

Selig, Robert. *The Washington-Rochambeau Revolutionary Route in the State of New York*. Hudson River Valley Greenway, 2001. www.hudsonrivervalley. org/themes/pdfs/rochambeau_revolutionary_route.pdf.

———. *Washington, Rochambeau, and the Yorktown Campaign of 1781*. Defense Dept., Army, Center of Military History, Center of Military History Publication, 2005.

Shonnard, Frederic, and Spooner, W.W. *History of Westchester County from Its Earliest Settlement to the Year 1900*. New York: New York History Co., 1900.

Simpson, Henry. *The Lives of Eminent Philadelphians, Now Deceased*. Philadelphia: William Brotherhead, 1859.

Sparks, Jared, ed. *The Writings of George Washington*. Vol. 2. Boston: Russell, Odione, Metcalf, Hilliard, Gray and Co., 1834.

Spikes, Judith Doolin, and Anne Marie Leone. *Irvington*. Charleston, SC: Arcadia Publishing, 2009.

Stanhope, Philip Henry Stanhope (Lord Mahon). *History of England, Vol. 7: From the Peace of Utrecht to the Peace of Versailles, 1713–1783*. Leipzig: Bernhard Tauchnitz, 1854.

Stone, Edward Martin. *Our French Allies*. Providence, RI: Providence Press, 1884.

Swanson, Susan Cochran. *Between the Lines: Stories of Westchester County, New York, during the American Revolution*. Pelham, NY: Junior League of Pelham, Inc., 1975.

Thacher, James. *Military Journal of the American Revolution*. Hartford, CT: Hurlbut, Williams & Co., 1862. Reprint, New York: New York Times and Arno Press, 1969.

Tuchman, Barbara. *The March of Folly: From Troy to Vietnam*. New York: Random House, 1984.

Unger, Harlow Giles. *Lafayette*. Hoboken, NJ: John Wiley and Sons, 2002.

Upham, Charles W., ed. *The Life of General Washington: First President of the United States*. Vol. 2. London: National Illustrated Library, 1851.

Weintraub, Stanley. *Iron Tears*. New York: Free Press, 2005.

Willcox, William B., ed. *The American Rebellion: Sir Henry Clinton's Narrative of His Campaigns, 1775–1782*. New Haven, CT: Yale University Press, 1954.

INDEX

ABOUT THE AUTHOR

R ichard Borkow is the village historian of Dobbs Ferry, New York, a trustee of the Dobbs Ferry Historical Society and editor of the website www.VillageHistorian.org. In 2009 and 2010, he was project director for *Noted Historians Reveal Dobbs Ferry's Historic River Connections*, a series of video interviews on YouTube with distinguished historians that was sponsored by the New York Council for the Humanities, the state affiliate of the National Endowment for the Humanities. He is a physician specializing in pediatric rehabilitation medicine and an attending at Blythedale Children's Hospital.

Visit us at
www.historypress.net